KU-694-944

"I'm seeing this big old world, the way it really is"

Four Thorns

by

The Chapters

THANK YOUS....

My Dad – when I was young you always encouraged me to read and when I was old enough, to write. Without you this book wouldn't have existed.

My sisters; Orla, Maria & Ciara – as a kid I always wanted a brother, as an adult I realise you had one all along, a very proud one!

Ray for trusting me with Shevlins Off Licence, where I wrote this – you really are stuck with me forever.

Orla for the Te Anau photo – www.orlaryan.com

Paul (Yaris), Gar, Eoin and Louise.

Ross from The Chapters.

Steven, Garrett and John from Original Writing/Writing4all.

This book owes everything to all I met along the way.
It's not about the place – it's about the people.
Rossi & Mick, Raymondo (rip), Anna, Ruxi, Mira, Jill, Miriam, John, Brownie, Cormac & Shane, Éilis, Caoimhe & Sandra, Mel, Malcolm, Oscar & Sam, Elliot, Lasse, Martin & Sarah from The Drunken Frog, Eve & Kate, Joergen & Søren, Kira, Lucy, Lee, Louise, Al, Kia, Ev, Vincent, Caroline, Ben & Daan, Shane, Sandra & Miriam, Jill, Panne, Catherine, Tom, Brian, Billy & Niall.

STORIES

DON'T TELL YOUR MOTHER

вackpacker tales

John Ryan

COMHAIRLE CHONTAE ÁTHA CLIATH THEAS
SOUTH DUBLIN COUNTY LIBRARIES
COUNTY LIBRARY, TOWN
TO RENEW ANY ITEM
OR ONLINE AT www.south

Items should be returned
as displayed in th

ORIGINAL WRITING

© 2010 John Ryan

www.backpackertales.ie

Cover photo by Steven Weekes

All rights reserved. No part of this publication may be reproduced in any form or by any means—graphic, electronic or mechanical, including photocopying, recording, taping or information storage and retrieval systems—without the prior written permission of the author.

978-1-907179-82-2

A CIP catalogue for this book is available from the National Library.

Published by Original Writing Ltd., Dublin, 2010.

Printed by Cahill Printers Limited, Dublin.

Music has always soundtracked my day and always will. The following soundtracked my writing day; One Day International, Gemma Hayes, John Mayer, Bell X1, The National, The Chapters and Michelle Doherty on Phantom. Thank you.

Mom, a sentence can't describe how great you are. No matter what I've wanted to do you've always supported me so this book is dedicated to you. You should stop reading now though, the following pages aren't stories for mothers!

Upload your own backpacker tale at *www.backpackertales.ie*

CONTENTS

Introduction

THAT PETROL EMOTION

I've always wanted to travel. I don't mean two weeks in the sun where by the end of it you look like a lobster and have drunk like a fish. I'm talking about places where the vodka tastes like a dairy product, where the healthy food is delicious and where the night-life blends into the day after the next.

When I left school I opted to work, unlike most of my friends who were college bound. A former maths teacher put it best when he called me aside one day and told me I was more into the social side of things rather then the academic side – I was 9. So always knowing this I wasn't too jealous of my friends' new college life. Yes, there were the parties, but there was also the college work. Exams, projects, assignments, presentations and usually balanced with a hazy hangover. Then the summer came and they were all gone, just like that. The kind of places that aren't weekend breaks in this part of the world: Rhode Island, San Diego, Vancouver. Stuck in my 9-5, I really was jealous.

Then, as they are unstoppable, the years rolled by. Bringing with them all the complications of getting older. Bigger bills, massive mortgages and that word you'd never heard when you were young – responsibility. But not only these emerged from life's lucky dip, it also brought fear.

It started small. I noticed one day I was afraid of heights. I couldn't believe it, looking over the top of a tall building had never affected me before, but now it had left me shaking. I think it's that little extra wisdom you gain and you start to realise you're as breakable as a child's toy. So you gradually get a little more settled in life, you have your comforts, you stick with them – you're happy. One day you catch the end of a travel programme. Tanned and beautiful, the presenter lists the merits of travelling to Vietnam and all you can think of is how you never got there. That was me at 30.

I know it's not easy just to leave and get on a plane. With all the excuses you build up in your head, it can actually seem impossible. I was now working as a project manager, a well paid job I enjoyed, and living in my own two bed apartment. I was doing well, had no serious debts to my name but at the same time no considerable savings. I still wanted to travel though, often talked about it after a few drinks, but with all that was going on in my life, I honestly didn't think it was possible. Then three things, *three little things* happened that eventually brought me to the city one Saturday morning to book a flight and face all my doubts head on.

There's a picture at the end of my bed. A photograph my sister took while on holiday in New Zealand. An old wooden pier stretches out onto the warm blue water of a lake. The far shore is surrounded by majestic mountains and a perfect cloudless blue sky oversees it all, smiling. The lake is Te Anau on New Zealand's south island. I used to look at this photo every morning – my house-warming present, but recently I found myself staring at it more frequently. I brought it into the sitting room. Outside the wind and rain made having a window an annoyance, I'd be inside for the day. Another look at the photograph. Inviting. I felt I had to walk on the old wooden pier.

With little else to do that day I really had no excuse but to do a much needed tidy. I am a hoarder, afraid of throwing anything out just in case it may be needed. I have no idea what possible use I may have for plastic kinder toys, old cinema tickets or a dozen mix tapes in the future, so I decided it all had to go. I filled a black sack as quick as I could so I wouldn't pause long enough to think of an everyday use for a broken toy gun. Nearing the end, it was old birthday cards that were getting the cut and here I noticed one. I remembered it straight away but hadn't thought about it for quite some time. It was from an ex girlfriend. The front showed different shades of purple outlining a tree. But it was the famous quote atop that I always loved. "The future belongs to those who believe in the beauty of their dreams." I didn't throw it out, I left it beside my New Zealand picture and went to bed with itchy feet.

A couple of weeks later I had just arrived home after a ten-day skiing holiday. I find Dublin airport the most depressing place to arrive back into and that was how I was feeling. It was Monday lunchtime and I just wanted to sleep before returning to work the next day. While I was away I had left my car in for a much-needed service so had to collect it before any sleep could be had. Having paid the mechanic I noticed I needed petrol so drove home via a garage. The driver in front of me clearly shouldn't have been driving on the road. At 20mph he swayed from left to right as if the excessive speed he was almost doing was causing havoc with the car's steering. Agitated I clenched my teeth and waited for the petrol station to creep up on the left. As it finally did, the car in front also indicated and very slowly turned. There were only two available petrol pumps, one after the other, and my inept leader pulled into the first, effectively blocking me from the final pump. A man, I'd guess in his 70s, climbed out of the car. I rolled down my window and politely asked did he mind moving forward so I could also get to a petrol pump. He looked at me, paused, then loudly said, "go around." I was taken aback by his abrupt rudeness. Fuming, I drove back onto the main road and in the far side of the garage. Before I could articulate the many expletives I was thinking, he chirped condescendingly, "see, that wasn't so hard."

"I thought at your age you would have learned some manners," I shouted.

He just smiled. A smile of a man defeated by what life had dealt him. Most of us cope and continue, he had crumbled. He had taken to live out his days as miserably as he had become and to hell with anyone around him.

Thank you, miserable old man. I know you would hate this, but that day you did a good deed. That day, before I fell asleep, I knew I was booking that ticket and still knew it after I woke up. *Three little things*. A picture, a birthday card, a miserable old man. That's all it took me to take that first big step and book a ticket. In the following months I handed in my notice and rented out my apartment. What seem like huge decisions while in your comfort zone, I can honestly say weren't. Sure, I was nervous, I thought about it all the time. What I was leaving behind, where I was going.

I think everyone should travel at some stage in their life. You'll just know when the time is right, I happened to be 30. Find your reasons, but if you don't, they'll find you. That picture, the friend that doesn't shut up about Australia, that dream. Believe in the beauty of your dreams. Don't be afraid. Walk out the door, catch that flight and embrace the places you've yet to see.

Chapter 1

DISCO INFERNO

Outer Mongolia

Through the right port-holed window all I could see was desert and, through the left, a perfect blue sky. The plane was making its final turn. 15 minutes and we'd be landing in Ulaanbaatar, Mongolia's capital, the pilot informed us. I stared out the window as the plane drew closer to the earth. Still nothing but sand. Apparently the airline I had paid money to for this view has the worst aviation record in history. That thought wouldn't leave my head as I continued to stare, a little uneasy now and a lot more sand, closer than before. Then, at what seemed the last possible second, tarmac appeared just in time for the wheels to make the connection. Having safely come to a stop I stepped off the plane. It felt like I had been wrapped in an electric blanket, such was the heat, and the taste of sand that swept up off the runway filled my mouth.

Instead of heading straight to the city I opted for the countryside, the Steppe as it is known here. About an hour from the capital, lies a small town called Zunn Mod. It is here a fellow Irishman had made his home and I was lucky enough to be offered a bed for the night and advice from a local. His girlfriend cooked up a feast for us which was washed down with the best tasting water I have ever tried, straight from the tap. It was surprising how ice cold it was while outside the sun could melt your flip flops right off your feet. Bottled and exported it might just be worth the ridiculous price we already pay for our branded water.

With the sun beginning to set we left the town and climbed a nearby hill. A view that I'd only previously seen on television greeted me, as we chatted and drank beer. The sun dropped and the moon rose to light up the night sky. Every few minutes shooting stars were spotted, then satellites would race from left to right, disappearing just as quickly. All the while the Milky Way was constant, resembling a single straight line of cloud. Imagine the M50 during a night-time rush hour – but in the sky.

The following day, accompanied by my new acting tour guide, we drove further into the Steppe. Roads are at a premium here and non existent where we were going so a 4x4 was a must. I was filled in on a few Mongolian traditions as our plan was to stay with a local family, but first we'd have to find them. Families living in the Steppe are like nomads, travelling around the countryside and setting up camp wherever they find suitable. After three hours of bumpy terrain we were beginning to lose hope until peering over yet another rolling hill, there in the valley below were three circular tents. Smoke emerged from the centre of one, confirming occupants. These tents are known as Gers (pronounced Gair) and provide shelter in Mongolia's harshest of winters where temperatures regularly drop to -40.

We approached the camp-site and were welcomed with firm handshakes and friendly smiles from faces that had experienced both extremes of weather. Straight away food was offered and we shared some very sweet and tasty Mongolian yoghurt. As the main meal was being prepared and the sun was beginning to set, we made our way to the top of the nearest hill for the best view. As my time here was limited I wanted to enjoy all the sunsets that I could. A cloudless, smog-free night sky is something I knew I wouldn't be seeing much of in the coming months. I stared in awe as the sky turned to pink then purple, rolling green hills spread out as far as I could see and off to my right I spotted the smoke from another Ger camp site. It was hard to get my head around the vastness of the countryside.

On our return a special treat had been prepared for us by an old woman who lived in a shoe, well actually, the opposite Ger. I'm guessing her age was close to 190 as she grinned toothless and nodded continuously at me. She handed me a small water bottle. The faded label may have suggested what it once contained if I had been able to read it but now it was filled with fermented mare's milk vodka. After smelling it I would have preferred the bottle's previous contents, old as it would have been. A crowd had now gathered around me and the old woman's nodding proved contagious, spreading like wild fire until I was surrounded by synchronised nodding Mongols. I rightly took it as a sign to drink up fast or there would be no dinner for me. Doing my best not to smell, I lowered half the bottle in one go then opened my mouth to try to avoid tasting and did my best not to get sick. Although this highly amused my on-lookers, they didn't budge until the bottle was empty. The nodding ceased, the crowd dispersed, I fell to my knees and desperately searched my pockets for a polo mint I might have forgotten from the '80s.

I crawled into the Ger as dinner was being dished out. There was a single bed to the right, what looked like a traditional Mongolian chest of drawers beside it with family photographs sat atop. In the centre a stove had been positioned so its long chimney exited through a hole in the middle of the roof. Quite homely, I thought, apart from the smell and look of dried meat that hung from the ceiling halfway round the room. What looked to me like spaghetti cheese tasted surprisingly like spaghetti cheese, which even more surprisingly was very tasty. I finished a bowl and then had a second.

Next a bottle of vodka was produced, luckily not from a mare this time, but from the chest of drawers, which turned out to make a better tasting spirit. Who'd have thought. The head of the Ger poured a shot and handed it out in the traditional manner. One hand holds the shot, the other touches the elbow. You accept the drink in the same manner and hand the empty shot glass back using the opposite hand. Getting into the spirit of things, literally, I graciously accepted the shots that were handed to me but soon realised the only thing that would bring this dance to an end would be an empty bottle or the passing out of one of the participants. The smart money was on me as with every shot my face contorted into new positions in an effort to swallow my poison. My drinking companion never once flinched. He may as well have been drinking Mongolia's latest exported bottled water. He showed compassion though, or just didn't want me to be sick on the floor of his house, and put the bottle away.

I had brought a Mongolian phrase book so we took turns in trying to make conversation. I learned the woman's name was Artha and she lived with her vodka-drinking husband and their three children. A daughter of 17 and two sons, 11 and 14. As I was flicking through my phrase book Artha tapped me on the shoulder. I glanced over and if I had any Mongolian words, I would have been lost for them. She was breastfeeding her daughter, who was 17, did I mention that? Artha gave me a wink, the daughter managed to suck and smile and I suggested the bottle of vodka should be reintroduced. All her children were still breastfed, it's just their way of life – a very different way of life as I was learning.

As the night progressed without any more feeding incidents, the children were sent next door to sleep in the neighbours. I had heard a story prior to my visit to the Steppe, which I didn't altogether believe. It was said that if the wife in a Ger takes a fancy to someone, she'll tell her husband to ask that person to sleep with her. I suppose, the Mongolian way of swinging, and now actions and pointing by the husband were directed at me.

A quick reference to my phrase book under the 'bizarre sexual habits' section confirmed my suspicions. Unfortunately it contained no advice on how to talk your way out of such a situation, only possible sleeping arrangements for a single bed that would contain her drunk husband. I managed a 'no thanks' and hoped by adding a thumbs up it would seem I was being polite. I zipped up my hoodie as far as it would go and pulled the strings so it tightened around my head. The temperature had dropped, but gazing through the gap in the Ger's roof at my favourite night sky sent me to sleep smiling.

The following morning it hit home that my diet isn't used to such sweet dairy products, as tasty as they were. Two weeks ago I had enjoyed my home comforts, particularly in this case, my toilet. But this was now Outer Mongolia, the middle of nowhere for someone from Dublin. I had a good scout around the area for a portaloo. I thought this might be where they were sent to save cleaning, after one of our outdoor concerts, but alas, was unable to locate one. So with an empty beer bottle filled with water and some local advice (pour with your left, wipe with your right) I walked as far away from the Ger as was comfortable. Taking position, watching vultures circle overhead, it occurred to me what a good quality of life we have back in Ireland, but the people here, not knowing any different, couldn't be happier or friendlier.

I spent the afternoon being taught how to handle a horse by an eleven year old. After witnessing the strength he possessed by taming a wild animal, I rather cleverly declined his offer of a wrestling match. If there's two things the Mongols can do, it's wrestle and drink, quite often together. It was time to thank Artha and her family and say goodbye. I gave her some money and she gave me that familiar wink. It had been a bizarre 24 hours and a great insight into a completely different world to what I'd known. I decided a good night's sleep back in Zunn Mod would be followed by a venture into the city.

Ulannbaatar

I woke up excited by not knowing what lay around the next corner. Today we were heading to Mongolia's capital, Ulaanbaatar. Arrangements had been made, we had the use of an apartment owned by Niall, another Irishman in Mongolia. Entering the city we soon realised that this is no holiday resort. In fact, up to recent years the number of tourists annually was only around 3,000. Hardly what you'd call a booming tourism industry and, believe me, this place needed an economic boost of some sort. Our accommodation lay at the far end of a cul de sac which hadn't seen Mongolia's blazing sun due to the high rise flats running the length on either side. Rubble crowded the street making driving in a straight line impossible. There was something very Russian about this place – war torn Russia.

After fighting over who had the first shower we left for a night on the town. The first stop for Irish lads is of course the Irish bar. 'The Dublin' claims to be Mongolia's first Irish bar but not the only one as less than two hundred meters down the road is a second. Unfortunately they weren't very clued in on our music as the thrilling choice of jukebox tunes were either Boyzone or Westlife.

With the realisation that we were actually only paying about 20 cent a drink, the night progressed rapidly and we found ourselves in a night club after a taxi ride. This probably isn't the best time to mention how stunningly beautiful Mongolian women are and it's not the drink remembering. Walk the streets to take in the culture and architecture and you'll no doubt find yourself looking waist high rather than sky high, they all seem to walk like models. Back in the club and I felt like Marco Polo having just discovered perfect skin, eyes, cheek bones and smiles. How are these women not gracing the pages of our typical men's magazines? As our conversation progressed nicely so did the dodgy looks I was getting from fellow clubgoers. The women might love talking to Westerners but the men aren't as interested. In fact, they loath you. With the music over, one of the more pissed and pissed-off Mongols started kicking my chair in an attempt to start something. Not getting the response he wanted he hit our Mongolian friend full pelt in the back and in return he received the need for a new dental plan courtesy of a drunken Irish 'handshake'. The alcohol seemed to quickly drain from my system with the sober realisation we were the only Westerners in a club full of unwelcoming Mongols. Amazingly I got my priorities right and gave the Mongol beauty my number before racing to find the bouncer.

Before I could even explain our slight predicament we were surrounded by drunk and what seemed now even bigger locals. One approached me extending an invite outside and, preferring the odds of a single Mongol to fifteen, I accepted. He declared he wanted $20 or he was going to call the police. Two things you want to avoid here due to bad practices and corruption are the hospital and the police. I had a horrible feeling I would be seeing one of those, but preferred the latter so declined the bribe.

Luckily at this point the bouncer allowed my fellow Irishmen out of the club and into an awaiting taxi for a speedy getaway, or it should have been except the taxi driver didn't move. The bouncer arrived to speed up proceedings with the due bribe. They exchanged money and instructions and we finally sped off but in the opposite direction to home. Realising the trouble in the club wasn't indeed over, just in the process of relocating, and not wanting to turn into a 'Missing in Mongolia' headline, we had to get out of the car. After refusing to stop we opened the back doors forcing the driver to slow down. When we escaped our death cab, the driver decided he wasn't finished and came at us armed with a can of mace and a police baton. We retreated to a nearby block of flats and decided it was safer to wait until morning before finding another, friendlier taxi. Everyone was shook up to say the least and the blame fell firmly on my lap which coincidentally is where she had been sitting.

Now for some travel talk. That particular night out, which included dinner, taxi transfers, club admission and a selection of drinks, excitement optional, came to €15. It certainly put my bribe offer of $20 in some perspective.

After summoning up enough courage to leave the apartment, it was time to see Ulaanbaatar during the day. Consulting my city map I found the National Museum of History. Admission was the equivalent of €5 but after confessing I would indeed be taking photographs while there, the price doubled. Suddenly I had forgotten my camera, in fact never even owned one, a digital what? €5 later I was wandering disappointingly through rooms displaying ancient hammers, stuffed animals, traditionally dressed mannequins and more hammers, of the modern type. Giddy with excitement now, I opted to leave, twirling my digital camera round my finger as I left. Oh, the simple pleasures!

Every July the Mongol Rally takes place inviting anyone with nothing better to do and who are comfortable for long periods in small spaces, to drive from London to Ulaanbaatar in any car under 1.2 litres as quickly as possible. These colourful cars had started to arrive and their occupants had started to make up for losing four weeks of their lives by drinking enough to have a further four-week hangover. I joined them for the annual table quiz which involved us confusing its rounds with our drink rounds. Soon a double vodka coke was the capital of Argentina and a new drink called a Buenos Aires was invented.

I awoke in a Buenos Aires haze the next morning, glad I'd made it home event free. I had met many friendly locals the night before, most offering to bring me on to their favourite nightclub, but, soured from my previous night, I always declined. This is a city in trouble. A mix of people who can afford to live, and people who can barely afford to exist. Walking the streets I often heard 'give me your money'. These people are beyond begging. There's no point, most are in the same state of poverty and there's very few visitors. The Mongol men like to drink and like to fight, that's their day made up. Then there's the street kids. Homeless and in most cases orphaned, they sleep under the streets beside the underground pipes for warmth to escape the deadly winters. I didn't feel safe and with every passing local eyeing me up, that wasn't female, I became more edgy. I needed to escape.

Stopping a passing car I headed for the train station. Any car on the road here is a taxi; these people have taken deregulation to the next level. I wanted to get to Beijing and I knew there was a train that goes all the way. Interestingly the train tracks in Mongolia and China differ so the train has to be lifted from one to the other at the border. Purchasing a ticket turned out to be very frustrating. The Mongols don't believe in queuing, they have mastered the technique of all piling forward until someone at the front is squeezed until they pop out at the available window. I was getting fed up of being squeezed and popped and then being told in perfect English that the English speaking window was the next one over. The guy in the last window who couldn't use the 'next window' excuse eventually got stuck with me amidst his snickering colleagues. I was bluntly informed the next available train going all the way to Beijing would be Christmas week. For a group of people that didn't want me in their country they didn't seem to want me to leave. I figured I could walk to Beijing quicker but would have to traverse the Gobi desert. Unfortunately I had mislaid my sunglasses the day before and therefore it would be utter madness.

Plan B would now have to be used but firstly thought up. Wherever you travel in the world and need help or advice, the local Tourist Information is not the place to go. You'll leave it with more leaflets than clothes in your expanding rucksack, a more confused head that's verging on a migraine and an impending need for beans and toast back in your hostel. Which in the end wouldn't be so bad because a hostel is exactly where you need to go. The staff are there to help and are used to all the problems and situations that can arise in their city for us globetrotters. Thankfully a train ticket was organised but I'd have to miss out on the changing of the tracks because this one would just take me to the border. I also booked a Chinese sleeper bus which would bring me from the far side of the border to Beijing in 15 hours. Now that just left the actual border crossing which couldn't be too difficult, could it?

It felt good to eventually close the door on the four-bed cabin in which I would spend the twelve hours overnight to reach the border. I was hot and tired but felt relatively safe so I opened the window and passed out. I'm guessing I slept for close to the twelve hours. When I opened my eyes I noticed the bedside table was covered in sand and not only that, so was I. The finest Gobi desert sand was embedded in my hair, eyebrows, ears and clothes. The Gobi is getting smaller and I'm to blame. Right on cue we arrived at the border station and I emerged from the train, Sand Trap Man. What confronted me was explosive mayhem. The contents of the train were being head hunted by Mongols with 4x4s promising safe passage across the border for several gold pieces. I had arrived into a movie scene and got to play the part of extra number 364, the one covered in sand. I spied two Israeli girls who seemed to be even more stupefied than myself. After joining forces we agreed on a fair price to break for the border, €10, which I based on the entrance fee for the club of the same name back home. The girls weren't impressed when I mentioned this, or maybe it was my new sand-do.

We drove into the desert and less then ten minutes later we were stuck in traffic. I thought maybe a set of traffic lights were faulty and stuck on red or someone might have double parked somewhere they shouldn't have. On closer inspection we had joined an existing line of 4x4s so the drivers could have a quick game of musical chairs and our new driver promptly asked for payment of €80. When I pressed the current matter of daylight robbery he enquired where I was from. He obviously wasn't up to date on the current economic downward trend making its way through foreign countries as he insisted, being Irish, I had plenty of money. Everyone involved in this epic border crossing was in the same boat, which was typical since we were in the middle of a waterless desert. We had no choice but to pay up and with that the rush hour traffic dispersed.

First stop was the Mongolian border where a mass ruck took place to squeeze through security, fill out our exit form and pay another €5 for the pleasure of it. Back into the 4x4 and on to the Chinese border where more form filling and security checks wasted a further hour in scorching heat before the final drive on to the nearest Chinese town.

I breathed a sight of relief and coughed up more sand. I had mixed feelings about Mongolia, there seemed to be a Heaven/Hell difference between the countryside and the city. Artha and her family seemed so long ago now but fresh on my mind was my nightclub experience. I threw my rucksack over my shoulder and smiled. It really was good to be alive.

Chapter 2

NOT FOR ALL THE TEA IN CHINA

Beijing

Having eventually made it inside China it was now time for some real Chinese food. As my sleeper bus was ready to leave it had to be a Chinese take away, of which I was familiar. So I sat atop my bunk bed, oblivious to all around in the five minutes it took me to devour my meal. Satisfied, I sat back and closed the plastic bag that held my now empty food container. It was then I noticed the bag was ripped and the five minutes of eating was also five minutes of grease leaking on to my army green shorts. Great, not only did I still have sand where there shouldn't have been, but I now looked like I couldn't find a toilet after a few too many pints. Not to worry, I thought, I'll sleep through the journey. I tried to stretch out but realised I'd grown too much in my 30 years, it was now time to go full circle and return to the foetal position. A bright red digital clock at the front of the bus seemed to taunt my efforts to sleep. In the darkness it appeared to scream out every slow passing hour.

With a jolt, the lights came on. 4am and we'd made it to Beijing. Not the best time to arrive, when I had no accommodation booked or any idea of my whereabouts. A French girl admitted she was equally clueless, so making a good match we found a taxi and headed to where we could find a hostel. We went through the 'not enough room at the inn' routine three times before we found a bed, or lucky for her, two beds. I was a very complementary mix of sand, grease and sweat at this stage but was too exhausted to care. With my last bit of energy I showered and then collapsed in a heap on a bed I fitted into.

Well-slept, I excitedly got dressed and bounded outside to see where I was in daylight. It was exactly what I thought China would be like, or exactly how it is portrayed in the movies in order for me to believe it should be exactly as it was. It was like walking down the street set in 'Indiana Jones'. Locals were cooking, eating, sleeping, and backpackers were enjoying the cheap beer. Turning the corner I arrived at Tiananmen Square, overlooked by the Forbidden City, which already had a considerable queue outside. I noticed most tourists that filled this area were Chinese. I was surprised at first but thought how big China is as a country. Some would have travelled 24 hours to get here. A digital clock at one end proudly counted down the arrival of the Olympics, not long now, just another year. A stage was being erected to celebrate later. Walking around I had the feeling I was being watched, in fact we were all under the watchful eye of the police who patrolled the square.

I joined the queue for the Forbidden City and attracted a new best friend. This is a very common scam throughout China so you need to be careful. Beside me now was a young Chinese 'student' asking me numerous questions about home and seeming very interested. They always pose as students on holidays, trying to be just like you, appearing helpful and friendly. Don't fall for it, it's just their sales pitch and I was waiting for mine. We finally finished queueing and entered the City. He then asked me to check out his art in his very own art gallery. Pretty impressive for just a student on holiday for the week. Then again I'd heard they were completing seven new underground rail lines in time for next year's Olympics – they do move quickly around here. Declining to invest in his art future I spent the next couple of hours getting lost in the Forbidden City's gardens and courtyards. I felt I'd walked the legs off myself by the end but had seen the same sight several times in different places.

It was mid-afternoon when I left and enough time to make the bank. I had made a fatal mistake the day I was leaving Mongolia. Wanting to withdraw the equivalent of €20 I accidentally pressed too many zeros and ended up with nearly €600 in Mongolian cash. My wallet wouldn't even close so I had to stuff my pockets with it too. The amused bank clerk looked on as I emptied my pockets and wallet in front of her and asked for the currency exchange.

"We don't take that money here," she smiled.

Surprised, I enquired as to the nearest bank that would.

"Mongolia," she replied, still smiling.

I laughed and then realised there was no joke, and no foreign exchange. Mongolia's economy is so bad no bank will deal with their currency. Since I wasn't going to go back to Mongolia I had to meet a Beijing-living Mongol who wanted to swap some funds in a brown paper bag – shouldn't be too difficult I thought. Back home a similar problem would have caused instant anxiety and stress, but here on the road, let loose on the world, problems didn't loom large on the horizon. Countless possibilities seemed possible. Although now in a situation where I knew less people in one place than ever before, I had a feeling that I could easily sort out any issue. I walked out of the bank and fell down the steps.

Being naive I thought the world spoke English, but not so. There are so many people living in China it's like a world on its own, with a thriving economy. They can play by their own rules of which there are many. There are a countless number of websites that can't be accessed here, including my own blog page, because the government has blocked them. If something big in the world happens you can bet your Mongolian currency that Google will be unreachable. There is even a website that lists all the sites that have been censored which I tried to check out but for some reason that too was blocked. Censorship is huge here. Its 'see no evil, hear no evil' policies, coupled with tough sentencing, make for an extremely safe city. I felt so safe I began to miss the danger involved in walking a dark Mongolian alleyway.

I laughed to myself when I thought back to the day I applied for my Chinese visa in Dublin. Not liking filling out forms of any kind means I'm not very good at filling them out. But as I ticked the 'Media' box as my current occupation, panic filled the room and a dozen more websites were blocked. The mouse pointer was held precariously over the 'Block Google and Initiate Shutdown Sequence' button as I clumsily explained I was in fact just stupid and thought m.e.d.i.a. was how you spelt manager. Chinese glared and locals sniggered but I mediaed, I mean *managed*, to avert an international world wide web disaster and with a bang of a rubber stamp was told to return in a week for my visa.

Despite the language barrier I had heard that if you're lost and hold a map out in front of you in the middle of the street you won't be long waiting for help. Well, that or get knocked down. Wanting to try out this theory I first bought a map. The next five minutes were spent struggling to unfold it. If only there were instructions and possibly a map to those instructions, it could have taken me half the time. Unfolded and with my best 'John's lost' facial expression, less then two pouts later and a helpful girl asked if she could help, because she was helpful. Realising I wasn't really lost I had to do some quick thinking. "Peking duck," I blurted out. Beijing is famous for this dish and I was always prone to Cantonese style roast duck from the local Chinese take away. She politely talked and pointed her way through the directions while her parents stood by smiling and nodding. It's mainly the younger generation here that speak English.

Not long later I was disappointingly eating a very tasteless duck. I was expecting something special, the real deal, but think my palate was too used to the added chemicals we get back home. Still, the map theory had worked, here I was. I thought of something else I'd heard. The Japanese are so honest that if you leave your wallet on the train, it'll be handed in to the nearest police station, cash intact. Similarly a story goes that someone dropped ten grand in notes on to a street and the majority of it was handed in. I was in no position to test that theory and didn't fancy risking even a €100. Besides, what was I thinking, I wasn't even in Japan.

Later that night I solved my cash problem. Drink in hand, I got talking to a Mongolian girl living in Beijing and now thanks to me, she also had a drink in hand. Outka told me she would be returning home for a visit the following month so didn't mind doing a bit of foreign exchange in the meantime. Our conversation continued and she admitted she hadn't yet seen The Great Wall, which was also on my to-do list. She mentioned she knew a driver that would take us there free of charge and after a quick call it was decided we'd exchange money and do some sightseeing the very next day.

We drove to Badaling where, in the car park, you can get a cable car right on to the historic wall. The historic point was made stale though as stalls and sellers surrounded us offering all kinds of tac. After fleeing them the wall was ours. On this part of the wall I think I was the only Westerner. Again the Chinese made up the majority of the tourists and they seemed to be as interested in me as they were in the Wall. They all smiled and said hello, stared and giggled at my hairy legs and the more adventurous asked me to join them in a photograph. I can see myself now, above the Wang's mantelpiece, the family portrait. Just me, Lín, Sóng, Yuán, and young Xú hanging out.

I truly loved Beijing. The friendliness of the place seemed to rub off on me and over the few days I was there I had many conversations with the locals. If only they had understood what I was saying. Still, they're so polite they can smile and nod with the best of them. I unraveled my map and decided it was time to find a train in the train station I was about to find.

Shanghai

Entering Beijing's train station was like passing through airport security. I queued to put my rucksack through the x-ray machine. When my turn arrived they weren't content to just x-ray my luggage but also wanted to see what was inside my recently purchased Burger King Whopper. Being in China this wasn't the sort of knowledge I needed. I made a point of checking the security guard's facial expressions. He didn't collapse on the floor laughing or have a good giggle with his colleagues so I ate away at probably one of the safest meals I've had. I then found my sleeper cabin and settled in for a snooze. There's something about the moving train that makes for a great sleep. The continuous 'clack clack' noise and gentle side to side sway.

I had studied my Shanghai guide book and therefore knew what to expect to pay for a taxi to my prearranged hostel. But, as I was getting accustomed to now, the driver quoted double. Although I'd never been here before, the best thing to do is pretend. I informed him I knew the city and had previously taken the same taxi ride. After he still put up a fight I told him to take me to the police station. This works a treat in China, and saving myself €20 I reached my riverside hostel. Luckily I checked in just before happy hour kicked off and after seeing the bar's prices, it would be the only time I'd be drinking there. The only redeeming feature was the fantastic view. A street away, the river passed below me and beyond that Shanghai's skyscrapers dwarfed the passing boats. At night, each of the buildings lit up, turning into gigantic televisions, impressively running adverts.

In the morning I went walking. The heat was full on but a dense cloud of smog blocked the view of the blue sky. I wondered when was the last time it had been sighted. I took the underground train to the far side of the river and made my way towards the Oriental Pearl Tower, which at a height of 468m offers the best view of the sprawling city. Already I was getting a much different feel to Shanghai as opposed to Beijing. A huge number of homeless, many of them physically deformed, begged for whatever they could get. The same art gallery owners did their best to poach passers-by, not as friendly as I had witnessed before but quite aggressive. At the entrance of the tower I paid my admission, joined the other tourists in the metal lift and we were rocketed to the top. The 360 degree views that awaited us were spectacular. Being from Dublin I was well impressed, then again what you're not used to will always seem impressive at first.

I made my way to the History Museum, which is in the city centre's park. With the museum in sight, two young and very beautiful Chinese girls approached. You know what's coming next – they were both students on holiday for the week to see the Shanghai sights and nights. We talked for awhile and even shared some ice cream, these girls were good! I was expecting to be asked to invest in some art once again, but it never came. Maybe these girls really were on holiday, isn't that possible? I told them I was going to check out the museum, to which they said they'd just been and didn't find it very good. Coincidentally they were on the way to a Traditional Chinese Tea party, and I was more then welcome. Being more stupid than welcome, I joined them.

I walked into what seemed more like a massage parlour, than a coffee shop, where I'd been used to drinking tea previously. Still, the ambience was nice and the oriental music and aromas seemed to filter away my doubts. We were shown to our own room, seated around a half-moon table and joined by two more tourists to complete the line up. Suckers Utd. For the next half hour a Chinese girl took us through the life stories and tales of eight different and seemingly mysterious teas. I never knew tea had played such a part in the progression of the human race. Apparently it started and ended wars, cured many a sick or wounded person and had the ability to make you a modern Don Juan de Marco. But sadly not one mention that it goes very well with an aul digestive biscuit. I imagined a cup of Lyons tea causing a dispute back home, resulting in years of drive-by shootings and burnt out homes, unraveling someplace outside of Dublin, let's say, Limerick – laughable.

After each story we were sparingly given one thimble of tea, just in case a war broke out in the very room if we drank too much. Mine was knocked straight back, hoping any moment women would started swooning, irresistible to me. But not so. The only desired effect it seemed to have, was to produce the bill. It was delivered by another girl who locked the door on her way out. Not a good sign I thought and the €130 bill confirmed that. It looked like tea was going to be responsible for another war after all. With great annoyance the bill was eventually paid, divided into five parts which included my two friends who had suggested the tea tasting. Afterwards we went for a drink and being so full after eight thimbles of tea I opted for a beer. I knew what had just happened had been a con, but I still wasn't completely convinced the girls were involved. After all, they paid their share and were now doing their share of bitching about tea. It was time for a shower and some food before the night took over so we exchanged pleasantries and numbers and I left for my hostel.

There it was, where it hadn't been hanging before. Newly written, meaningful and in an aggressive tone. You could tell the author wasn't to be messed with at the time of writing. I read the words, each sentence they made up, stabbed me. My blood pressure rose and I felt my face redden. "Beware of Traditional Chinese Tea Tasting Con", the headline read. This I knew, but the following description included my girls, the students on holiday. I felt stupider than Jupiter. I knew what to avoid and still got done. How many backpackers were taken up the tea path? Why wasn't there a warning in my guide book? Do we do the same to tourists back home?

This is a cup of Lyons tea and this is a cup of Barry's. One can instantly cure the worst of hangovers, the other can make you fly. That will be €200 and your watch please.

I showered, changed, and pleased I did this in the right order I ventured out to Shanghai at night. I stopped at a street corner, ordered some chicken fried rice from a vendor and sat uncomfortably on a child's plastic chair, opposite the matching table. It was like I was attending my two year old niece's tea party and tea was the last thing I wanted to think about. Luckily the freshly cooked food was fantastic and cost less then a Euro. After, I found a street with a bit of life caused by a number of bright neoned bars. I noticed I was getting a lot of female attention straight away, maybe the mysterious tea qualities were beginning to kick in. It didn't take me a full drink to realise I was in a 'women of the night' bar. On leaving, it was apparent it wasn't just the bar, but the whole street. To fit into what I thought about Shanghai so far, they were quite aggressive too. While hailing a taxi I was surrounded by women, it was sale of the century, come on down, the price was right. I jumped into the front seat of a passing taxi and three girls took the opportunity to jump in the back. After assuring the driver they weren't with me he seemed to take pleasure in physically removing them.

The taxi stopped outside a spectacular looking club. Its architecture wouldn't have been out of place beside Rome's Pantheon. The low thud of a bassline sonically came to life as I opened the taxi door. A neon blue hue coated the club's exterior giving the queueing partygoers the appearance of smurfs. A good crowd lined the bar on the left, occupied the seated area in the middle and stood around a single pool table on the right – game in progress. I ordered and was given a drink and made for the pool table. A chalk board made up of mainly Chinese names listed those awaiting to play, so I added my name. I got talking to an American couple and several double drinks later it was his turn to play pool. He turned out to be pretty good to the dismay of the Chinese crowd and, unable to beat him decided he wasn't allowed to play anymore. After inquiring as to why I wasn't allowed play either, I found myself flat on my back having been pushed over a table and chairs. Between the roars, shouts, threats and more pushes, a Chinese girl advised us to leave as the owner of the club was among the Chinese crowd, who apparently wasn't to be messed with. Clearly not thinking straight I ushered the couple out of the club and into an await-ing taxi to safety. I, on the other hand, opted for danger or in this case stupidity, and went back inside.

What happened next are snapshots of memory, pieced to-gether now, when I think back. There's no continuous path, just jumps in time to different faces and places.

I bought a drink and spoke to several people at the bar, in-cluding I'm sure of it, the owner himself. Not remembering leav-ing, I am now on the streets of Shanghai, it's late and I'm not alone. My companion is a Chinese girl, early 20s and I'm talk-ing the ear off her. I'm not sure she understands, I know I don't. There's nothing after that, just blankness. Then something hits me in the head and my eyes open just in time to see my second shoe smack me square in the nose. Extending my gaze, I can see the Chinese girl isn't happy. Throwing my shoes at me didn't vent enough anger, she's pacing now and speaking in tongues unknown, I'm guessing Chinese. After a few attempts my shoes go on. I have them set for 'lazy mode' so the laces never need to be tied, just as well because I'm sure now I couldn't do them. I stand up and want to get out of there before the angry girl starts throwing any other available objects. I know I'm not right. The thought of getting the girl's number doesn't even enter my head, a bad sign. I stumble out into the daylight, my legs are work-ing, but I'm not sure how. I guess it's about 8am, maybe earlier. High-rise flats surround me on all sides. The way I face is the direction I move so I point myself to what looks like a main road. There's about ten or more people waiting at a bus stop. I scan each of their faces, going from one to the next, they each look at me weirdly. I feel weird and know I couldn't handle a bus. I walk past them and stand out on the road, praying for a taxi. I check my pockets. My wallet and hostel key are still there. A taxi pulls in and as I collapse into the passenger seat things start to go blank again. I can think fine, in my head I know what's going on. I know this is no hangover, I've had one or two of those before. The taxi driver wants a destination and now I realise I can't talk. The cat has taken my tongue, given it to the dog and he's buried it at the end of the garden. I see the sentence in my head but that's where it stays. I pass out.

I awake as the taxi driver pulls me up from the passenger seat and out of the car. He's brought me to the hospital I think to myself, but looking around it's just a busy street, rush hour traffic, people going to work. He positions me sitting down, my back against a shop window, retreats to his taxi and drives off. If, at home, you find yourself on O'Connell Street, your back to Easons, 8.30am Monday morning and unable to move – you're in trouble. Now here I was in aggressive Shanghai. I black out and am woken by a passing Chinese, inquiring if I am okay. I'm still unable to talk, I do my best to politely nod, always remembering my manners, before passing out again. This happens several times but each time I gain consciousness I feel a bit more strength returning to my limbs. A plan formulates through the fuzz. My hostel key is handily attached to a hostel keyring, naming my destination. I just need to stand, walk the width of the path and hail another taxi. After another cat nap this is what I do. The hostel door was luckily ajar and I staggered through it. My walk had returned but my head had started to pound helping the nauseating feeling build up in my stomach. I have never been so happy to see a hostel bed. We were acquainted until the following morning, when at last my appetite had returned.

I think back on that night. Pin-pointing my mistake is easy, I shouldn't have gone back into the club, but I'm sure my drink was never out of my hand or eye shot. I'm convinced my drink was spiked behind the bar. The angry shoe-throwing Chinese girl, whoever she was, may well have saved me that night. In the state I was in, Shanghai is the last place you'd want to be wandering aimlessly. I packed up and without reluctance returned to the train station to leave Shanghai. I had been stupid, but lucky the outcome wasn't worse. The train's 'clack clack' seemed like sweet music that night as it gently rocked me to sleep.

Hong Kong

I awoke as the train started to slow down. It was approaching Hong Kong. Secluded inlets and rolling rich green hills gave way to the city skyline of tightly packed skyscrapers. The English influence was evident all around. Taxis were now uniform red and street names like 'Arsenal Street' appeared. My accommodation search prior to my arrival confirmed this wasn't a city for backpackers on a budget. I eventually found a reasonably priced room on Hong Kong island, my preference over Kowloon. I took the underground and was immediately impressed. Apart from being very well signposted, making it impossible to get lost, this place was spotless. Either they had excellent around the clock cleaning staff, or nobody here littered.

It didn't take me long to find the street my accommodation was on, but I was having real problems trying to locate the building. They seemed to have crammed an impossible amount of people into one space, occupying homes and businesses. With a little help I was directed to a door I had already passed three times. A small sign told me I'd be staying on the 46th floor. Upon seeing my room, I thought crammed was too nice a word. I had to take my rucksack off to squeeze through the door, a fitted single bed faced me and there wasn't enough floor space for myself and my rucksack to stand together. By placing my baggage on the bed and turning sideways, I could open the toilet door. It felt like a round in the Crystal Maze. 46 floors up and no windows, I couldn't make up my mind which name was more suited, a cell or a shoebox.

I set out to explore the city and was enjoying checking out the numerous different stalls that lined the streets and alleyways, when I spotted a sign advertising 'Ear Candle'. My curiosity got me through the door and up to the counter, a beautiful girl brought me the rest of the way. I was laid out on a masseuse table and told to relax as the girl fumbled through an adjacent closet. Happy with her findings she turned smiling, holding up a long, thin, white candle and a zippo lighter. Before any questions could be asked she had stuck the candle as far into my ear as she could jam it and lit the end. She then hurriedly left the room. The sound was loud, familiar, and getting closer. The A Team flashed into my head. Why? That familiar sound – a stick of dynamite. Now I know it was a ridiculous thought, but nonetheless I could see the sparks jumping off the candle as it burned down, nearing my ear. As images of my head exploding filled my mind, the girl returned and removed the candle. After showing my other ear the same attention she then cut open the remaining pieces of candle and proceeded to give out to me. I apparently had too much wax in my ear and was a very bold boy, her broken English told me. I thanked her for not blowing up my head and left to try out the new super-human hearing I must have acquired. I narrowly avoided a bus while crossing the road; I hadn't heard it coming.

Hong Kong is in the Guinness Book of Records twice, so I decided to check out both. Firstly, it has the longest running light show, starting at 8 every night and lasting 15 minutes. I took centre stage down by the harbour, surrounded by Hong Kong's tall buildings and just across the water from Kowloon's skyscrapers. The music started, dramatic, orchestrated, but losing all its substance due to the poor quality speakers pushing it out into the night sky. The next 15 minutes seemed like 30. The building's rooftop lights flashed on and off, changing sequence, trying to keep up with the increasingly annoying music. I noticed a family to my right visibly in awe, I presumed they didn't get out much or even at all. I suppose just because it made the record books didn't have to mean it was any good, just that it was there. There it was so there I went.

Needing some perking up after that, the second Guinness Book entry seemed a lot more appealing. The longest outdoor escalator. Here's the magic. Situated on a steep hill, during the day it descends, bringing people to work and at night it ascends bringing people to the many bars and restaurants. Since I didn't have a job here, I had to be content with the nightlife. The packed bars overflowed on to both sides of the street, the stunning women making it look like a slanty catwalk. Music pulsed from each bar and a short walk was like flicking through different radio stations. I was enticed into one by a live band. An r'n'b song turned into rock, the guitar solo defined, then disowned, the melody. Drinks weren't cheap and it didn't take much more than a glance to attract the working girls' unwanted attention.

The next day I decided to check out Ocean World. You'd be forgiven for thinking this was a water park, as I did, but it's actually a giant theme park. Not the biggest fan of these rides but having paid the entrance, I decided it was time to get scared. I found 'The Abyss', which, being the tallest object here, couldn't be missed. A 200m drop strapped to a chair isn't usually my cup of traditional Chinese tea but I was soon shoeless and in position. We were slowly lifted from the ground, the view getting better, the nerves getting worse. Having made the total ascent we stopped. The drop was seconds away, but which second? Anticipation built up, we dropped from the sky. The seats were no longer in use, the shoulder straps held us in against the G forces. We hit the bottom, screaming and laughing faces met for an instant before we bounced halfway back up again, like a giant spring. I was finally reunited with my shoes.

Returning to the city streets I sorted out my visa for Vietnam, which I had decided would be my next stop. The Vietnamese embassy was extremely efficient and within 30 minutes my passport was stamped and ready to go. If the friendliness of these people was anything to go by, I was in for an exciting month.

Chapter 3

SAIL AWAY

Hanoi

Before leaving for the airport I booked my hostel on line. Hanoi Backpackers seemed like the right place to stay after reading the comments of praise left by numerous other happy backpackers. I promptly received a reply email from them outlining a common scam that takes place. Awaiting taxi drivers not only overcharge to take you into the city but they will also try to persuade you the hostel you booked is full, opting to bring you to one they know instead, collecting a nice commission themselves. Due to this, Hanoi Backpackers offers a private taxi service from the airport for just $12, which I accepted.

I noticed the sign first, 'John Ryan – Hanoi Backpackers' and then my gaze fell upon who was holding it. With a smile, I approached and introduced myself and was met with a very enthusiastic handshake and offers to carry my baggage. We left the airport together and found his parked car. While loading my rucksack into the boot I noticed what looked to me like a nitro, and at the speed we took off, I'm sure it was. My driver had placed his baseball cap on backwards and while he weaved at speed through the traffic he talked about his hero, who not surprisingly, was Michael Schumacher. The increasingly alarming observation was that he looked, at the most, 14. Certainly not old enough to have a driver's licence, and drove with all the gusto of a child after stealing his father's car keys.

The hostel itself is situated in the Hoan Kiem District, not far from the lake that dominates the bustling city and, after thanking my young driver, I checked into my Australian-owned accommodation. The important rules were first explained. Happy hour was on every day from 5 in the rooftop bar, where I could also avail of three free barbecues a week, including a free keg of beer on Sunday, which, I presumed, I'd have to share.

Having availed of the happy hour, my new Canadian friend suggested a visit to the local Irish bar. I've always thought Irish bars are fantastic – when they're not in Ireland. They represent what our bars used to be like until a clever somebody suggested giant urns and over sized lampshades that could conceivably accommodate their very own bar. Looking forward to a bit of Irishness in Vietnam I was disappointed when we came across the closed shutter. Having seen this before though, my friend simply knocked. Out of the shadows appeared a kid, similar to my driver, but this one had been entrusted with a zapper. After a quick look around for the unapproving, the shutter rose enough for us to enter and let the smell of cabbage and potatoes out into the night sky.

Things had really kicked off here and the locked shutter seemed to give the revellers an extra safety and belief that maybe this party might never end. The bar on the left and tables on the right gave way to the pool area – that of the table persuasion. Young people of all ages, except old, dressed like they were at a pool party – that of the swimming type. The walls were covered in writing, like ancient cave drawings, passing on travel tales and advice. "Don't cry cause it's over – smile cause it happened," caught my eye. U2 were still looking for something they still hadn't found after possibly losing it in a place like this and as I approached the bar, a girl approached me. A man already there had just ordered six pints of Guinness but appeared to be alone.

"Are you Australian?" she asked me in a Dublin accent.

Delighted my tan had really come on that much, I told her I was also from Dublin. With a look that equally registered disappointment and disgust, she threw her nose in the air and walked off. The man next to me chuckled to himself. I noticed only three pints remained.

The next morning I awoke with a head like a Jackson Pollack. The bar had finally let me leave but was by no means closing at that stage. I left the hostel to take in Hanoi in daylight. Immediately the small streets appealed to me, giving the large city all the cosiness of an open fire-heated sitting room. I reached the lake and was stunned at the amount of motorbikes, a continuous flow of them, both sides of the road. Beijing may be all about the bicycle, but Vietnam is king of the old motorbike. Luckily the helpful hostel owner had educated me on the safe-cross-code 'Nam style'. The thing to do is to walk slowly onto the road and keep that pace until the other side, the idea being that they'll simply avoid you. Knowing this though, it can still be quite unnerving the first time, trying to resist the urge to make a run for it. I witnessed an American woman who hadn't quite grasped the concept as she barrelled out onto the road, marginally missed the first moped before taking out the following four. Those lucky enough to survive the road get to enjoy the vast and beautiful lake. Although it acts like a giant roundabout, the thousands of motorbike engines can't take away from the peace and calm felt all around it. Suitably, at the closing of the day, it's here where yoga enthusiasts gather and the fit get fitter. The countless unbroken tail of headlights in the dark seemed like a protective blanket, keeping us all tucked away, safe inside.

Taking a walk around the streets and markets will endear you to this city even more. Anything you could want is on sale here and for cheaper than you think. The Vietnamese Communist revolutionary Ho Chi Minh is embalmed here in the Ho Chi Minh Mausoleum, modelled after Lenin's Tomb in Moscow, despite his wishes to be cremated. Knowing Time Magazine had named him as one of the 100 most influential people of the 20th century and the Vietnamese people had renamed their capital in his honour, I thought it worthwhile to join the silent queue to take a look. The guards forbid you to speak out of respect and any photographic equipment has to be checked in. Then you're marched slowly in line up a stairs, through the room in which he is laid to rest and out the other side, where they let you talk again. He looked like he *was* just having a rest and we were being quiet so as to not to wake him. He's been dead since 1969.

Thinking it was time for food and not too early for beer I stopped at a street-side diner. Well, I suppose, dinner at the side of the street is more accurate. Similar to China, miniature plastic table and chairs were produced, suitable for ages 3-5, available from Mothercare. A feast was prepared as quick as a drive-thru McDonalds could be bought and without any of the fast food side effects. Healthy food at its most delicious. I thought the food was cheap until I discovered Vietnam's Bia Hoi, or 'fresh beer' at the very cheap price of only 15 cent. 90 cent later I fell off my chair but managed to escape severe injury after my mere 12-inch descent to the ground.

Later on, and still feeling the effects of my new found tipple, I decided to check out Hanoi's famous water puppets, which take place in an old theatre with the stage covered in water and a live band playing traditional Vietnamese instruments off to the side. Over the next hour puppets fought each other, avoided dragons and found love, all played out to a different song. I thought the whole thing was a bit freaky but quite entertaining for the hour.

Rejoining others from the hostel, we were off to a nightclub and the quickest way to get around is, of course, by motorbike. Anybody will give you a lift for a small fee. It soon became a race. Prices were shouted at our drivers to get them to go faster, win bonuses promised for getting to the club first. With so many motorbikes here it's surprising to see only a small percentage of helmets. The government is trying to make them compulsory due to the increasing fatalities, but this statistic was as far from our minds as the ground was to our helmetless heads while we raced through the dark streets, banter bouncing from bike to bike. We arrived at the club and outside a group of local men were huddled, arguing close to a slumped body. Head wounds were obvious. He had come off his motorbike at speed, no helmet. Time passed and still he lay there, no medical attention and no ambulance. The local men finally came to an agreement, picked him up and placed him in the back of a taxi – another statistic.

The following morning in my hostel I booked two trips. Firstly, I would head north on an overnight sleeper train to do a two-day trek in Sapa and after that it was on to Halong Bay, where the enticing-sounding Paradise Island awaited. But before that I still had a spare 30 cent to spend.

Sapa

Well slept, the following morning we were transferred onto a mini bus that took us the remainder of the way to Sapa. The scenery exploded as we made our way higher up the mountain pass, into and beyond the clouds. All the greenery to match Ireland spread out below us and even our weather seemed to be replicated. A misty rain not so much fell as surrounded us, leaving us soaked to the skin in no time.

After an hour we came to a standstill. Traffic jams in remote parts of the world were becoming all too common. On closer inspection an important part of the equation had been subtracted – the road was no longer there. The recent bad weather softened the soil, causing a landslide. Nature, being creative and having an eye for decorative gardening, had placed boulders in a circle, surrounded the feature with sand and then added water to create a pond. I was all but waiting for a urinating statue to plummet to the ground, becoming the prearranged centrepiece. The locals didn't appreciate Nature's effort, though, and soon the bulldozers had arrived to reclaim their much-needed road. It wasn't long before we reached our destination and I met my tour guide, suitably named Nam. He explained, due to Sapa being at the very top of a mountain, the weather was usually wet and cold but once we descended to the valley floor the hot sun would surely melt us. With great excitement we set off. I was looking forward to some tough exercise since I hadn't even been for a run since I left Ireland.

It started off easy. The path was good enough so you could enjoy the view, you weren't completely out of breath and you could chat. But the paths turned to muddy inclines and the streams to rivers. It didn't take long to realise I didn't have the proper footwear in runners. The soles were now so caked in mud it gave me an extra couple of inches in height but took away any grip. I gave up on the idea of staying any way dry and ploughed on. Nam mentioned that most of the other treks that were to depart that day had been cancelled due to the bad weather, but he believed we could handle the bad terrain. I was seriously beginning to curse his belief in us and doubt his character judgement call.

Luckily a group of local girls, know as Black Hmong tribeswomen, had joined us by now. We appeared to be heading in the direction of their village. They masterly traversed the increasingly impossible terrain making it seem they had specially made feet, or at least footwear. I took a closer look – they were wearing wellies. As the overall conditions worsened I found myself on a muddy ledge. A Paddy field to my right, waiting to cover me in leeches upon entering, and a cliff to my left, waiting to kill me upon falling. Panic set in and then the realisation that health and safety doesn't exist in this country, which in turn worsened my panic. Two of the girls took a shine, which was probably closer to pity, for me, since I was struggling at the back. With surprising strength they each took a hand and helped me maintain my balance until we'd reached safer ground. I proceeded to repeat 'thank you's' like they were the only two English words I knew. I enquired as to how old they both were. "13," they replied. What is it about strong children over this side of the world? I gave them some money as thanks but also as a bribe not to tell my friends back home what had just happened. You never know who's on Facebook these days.

We drew closer to the valley floor and, as Nam had said, the temperature soared and t-shirts became headbands. In late evening we entered a small village in search of our accommodation for the night. Rounding a bend I was faced with a make-shift sign. Four words had been written in red paint and at that point, being exhausted and hot, I don't think there were four greater words in the English language. It simply read "Welcome! For Cold Drinks." I bounded up the steps, into the fridge and emerged with indeed, cold beer. My Mongolian water.

After pretending to rehydrate myself, it was time for a wash. It was getting dark now and there was no light in the cement cubicle shower. Having used a shower before, in fact I'd go as far as saying I've had so many showers down through the years, I'm a shower expert, I felt around in the dark to where I'd usually find the 'produce water now' knob. With no luck I ascertained that Asians are generally not as tall as Westerners so the shower knob must be lower. I searched lower, then lower still. Finally my hand grasped a tap, it was at knee level and just below that a bucket with a soup ladle inside. I did my best to dollop myself with cold water in-between bursts of tears and crazy laughter.

Ordealed out for one day I sat and enjoyed what was, at last count, a 12-course feast. Vietnamese cuisine is fantastic. All the ingredients were grown a potato's throw from my table, cooked to healthy perfection and devoured with a broad smile. I got to the stage I was so full I couldn't eat any more but it was so delicious I couldn't bare to part with my plate. I argued with a spring roll for awhile, ate half of it and went to bed. Then got up quickly, ran back to the table in a panic, graciously ate the other half and returned to bed. Wrapped in a mosquito net cocoon I slept until I woke the next morning.

We took a vote and decided we were too lazy and still too full so we'd hitch a ride on the backs of motorbikes out of the valley. As we climbed higher the view grew more impressive. I had to hold on tight to the bike as gravity gave me the feeling the village was trying to pull me back to live there. We made it back to Sapa and the Irish weather in the late afternoon. Having finally digested yesterday's food it was time to enjoy more. Afterwards I bade farewell to Nam, thanking him for our 27km adventure. I had another overnight train to catch back to Hanoi, where a bus waited to bring me to Halong Bay and the promising-sounding Paradise Island. I wondered did they serve cold beer.

Halong Bay

Disembarking from the bus I gazed upon about 20 wooden boats, each with enough accommodation for 30-plus people. Tourism is big business in Halong Bay and like a cattle mart we were herded and equally distributed among the boats. Pirates are common, silently boarding the boats at night while they are anchored in the bay, plundering the wares of the sleeping beauties and then departing as quickly. Explain that to your insurance company. I had no need to worry though, I wasn't going to be spending a night at sea. Paradise Island awaited me far off on the horizon. An island populated entirely by exotic females in straw skirts. Starved of males and feeling the ticking of their biological clocks, they would be serving me cocktails and fanning me to sleep on my hammock. I presumed this is what the brochure would have said if the hostel had any left. Not to worry, I'd soon find out, but first there were caves to explore.

Yet another traffic jam, this time on water, indicated we had travelled the short distance across the bay and arrived at the caves. We waited for our turn to dock and then began to climb the countless steps to the entrance. Progress was slow as everybody got the urge to take numerous identical digital photos at the same time, just in case the last one didn't turn out right, even though they had just checked on its perfection. I resisted the temptation until the very top. I turned around, caught my breath, let it go, and then remembered how to breath normally again. The view was picturesque perfect. Mountains on either side secluded the inlet, thus making it into a bay. The crystal flat water was interrupted only by the soft ripples made by more boats arriving. The weather framed the view and I took a photograph to freeze the moment. It now hangs on my bedroom wall.

Ten minutes and I was already in and out of the cave, left with a disappointment of cavernous proportions. I suppose that's the thing about most caves, the ones you can easily and safely walk around are just boring. Large stone, echoey rooms. Exciting caves involve a fair deal of crawling on your hands and knees, often in the dark, giving you a sense of confusion and a fear of being lost and forgotten. The threat of a cave-in at any minute, I find, is also good to add to the experience.

Back on the boat, a course was set, full speed ahead engaged – then we stopped. A smaller boat had pulled up alongside us and all destined for Paradise Island were ordered to walk the plank, which luckily led onto the other boat. All aboard, I counted our resized crew. Five. I re-counted. Still five. Myself, two other males and a couple. I figured Paradise Island must be nearing its party capacity so we were the final lucky ones. The captain knew an able seaman when he saw one and ordered me to take charge of steering our small vessel.

"Aye aye captain," I replied but he was already asleep in the shade, leaving one sucker in the sun. Two agonisingly slow hours later and on the verge of sun stroke, I shouted "land ahoy," and woke the captain much to his disgust. Indeed there was land but due to our top speed it was still at least a further two hours away.

Two and a half hours later we were finally docking. We'd made it – party time. We were greeted by two Vietnamese guys, one in charge of the bar, the other the food.

"How many other people are on the island?" I enthused.

"Just you five," came the reply.

The five of us looked at each other. We all knew we had used up most of our conversation on the boat getting here. Now, faced with three days together, on a small island, which was really just a beach, we'd have to think of something quick. Our combined quick-thinking found us at the bar. An urgent need to get drunk had been acquired by us all, so cocktails were on the menu.

First I ordered a Harvey Wallbanger. Usually of the orange colour, I was surprised when it arrived the colour red. That was soon followed by a Pina Colada, which too was red. A quick glance down the bar confirmed all the cocktails were red and they had obviously run out of certain ingredients that weren't red. To lighten the mood, even to a lighter shade of red, we decided on a game of pool. Attempts to prove any of us could actually play were hindered by a sand trap at one end of the table and severe flooding the other. Playing around the obstacles soon became tiring so we retired to some nearby couches. Sitting there I realised I was annoyed because something was annoying me. It wasn't the strangely coloured cocktails or the assault course pool table, it was in fact the music. More to the point, the music hadn't changed since we got there and as rubbish as Jack Johnston was prior to arriving here, repeated listens to his album made him no better and the listener close to psychotic. Paradise Island sank to a new low when I discovered a change of music was as hard to find as certain cocktail ingredients. Not nearly drunk enough, but with lips like I had been guzzling red wine since early morning, I found bed.

I awoke to a loud bang and a flash of light. My first thought was that a fat photographer had fallen down some nearby steps, but realised after it happened again, a fierce storm was playing itself out centre stage on the water. The thunder grew louder as the storm approached our little island in the dark. Forked lightning appeared to cut the world in two, one half blue, the other purple. In one of its great flashes I spotted our small boat dancing back and forth as the waves pushed and pulled it into a state of confusion. When the storm exited stage left my eyes shut once again and I slept.

By early morning, cabin fever had started to affect me. I needed a break from paradise, even for a few hours, so I hitched a boat ride to Cat Ba, the neighbouring island with considerably more inhabitants. I decided I'd first treat myself to a shave as I'd grown lazy the last few days. The first shop window offered men's haircuts and shaves and looking further inside, four beautiful girls were on the payroll. I walked in to smiles and giggles which promptly stopped when I explained I wanted a shave. By the time I'd taken a seat, three of the girls had disappeared into the back, and the fourth through the front door. I sat, waited, and looked around. Only then did I notice the unusual items adorning the shelves. Items not usually found in a barber's. A litre bottle of Jack Daniels, a selection of beers and a cocktail mixer. Realising the women employed here were probably involved in a different kind of male grooming, I got up to leave just as the fourth girl returned with a bemused male in tow. I gathered she had left in search of someone who really did work in a barber's. I announced my new intentions of growing a full beard instead and left.

Bored with the beard plan shortly after, I found a legitimate barber's and settled back into the chair. Things started to go wrong pretty quickly as shaving foam was applied to my face without any water beforehand. The girl nominated by the boss to execute me took a deep breath before placing the blade on my neck. I closed my eyes, bracing myself for pain. By the time I'd reopened them she had a very confused look on her face and her eyes were shouting to her boss for help. Not good. She disappeared into the back, embarrassed and in fear of having killed yet another tourist. The boss then took over, skilfully working his way around the box of tissues he'd applied to my skin and finished up with a peace offering of a cup of tea. Afraid to look in the mirror, I stepped out into the sunlight, my neck burning raw.

After eating possibly the best chicken fried rice ever made, which momentarily took my mind off the pain, I decided I'd rent a motorbike and see the rest of the island. Motorcycle rental here is easily done. No forms to fill out, no ID required, no deposits taken. You simply walk out onto the street, spot a local with said bike and make him an offer. $20 got me a few hours and no helmet so to coordinate my outfit I removed my t shirt. I took off like a rat out of a bell who was in fear of going deaf. I should mention, previous to this I was never in control of a motorbike before, but it wasn't long until I had the basics down and the revs up. A cool breeze soothed my raw neck as I took to the coast road. It felt like I was driving on a ledge that had been chiselled into the cliff, halfway down. I could hear the waves slap against the rocks below. I changed gear, rounded a corner and narrowly avoided a snake who was out for an afternoon slither. The road was mine but it felt like the whole island was too. The sun warmed my bare neck and shoulders and time seemed to have no meaning. A glance at the petrol gauge though was enough to remind me of time's powerful grasp over man and a bike's need for fuel, so I directed it back towards its owner.

I walked the pier and found the small boat that would return me to pure paradise. No sooner had I stepped on, than the owner stepped off. I thought he may have caught sight of my blood-dry neck but then he mentioned something about ingredients and ran off. I hoped he was referring to the cocktails. I sat on the open top boat and waited, enjoying the gentle sway the waves provided. The rope that kept the boat tied to the pier was now at full length, creating a good five metre gap between the two. As if sensing a trapped Irishman, a swarm of hornets descended on the boat. Not being a fan of wasps, their more aggressive relation terrified me. I bolted all of 6 foot to the other end of the boat but after sending out a search party, they found me again. I armed myself with my t shirt but realised it just gave them more skin to aim for, so I put it back on. I invented a new dance, arms waving madly, legs kicking out like a drunken horse as my head shook along to an unheard beat. Acting like a possessed kangaroo I hadn't noticed I wasn't alone any more until the small engine was started and its owner directed us towards the island with a bemused look on his face.

Back on the island little had changed so with little else to do I decided to take a kayak out for a paddle before dinner. This was another first for me, but in the calm blue water facing the beach it was easy to get into and keep a good rhythm going with the oar. It didn't take me long to get my confidence up, and feeling I'd graduated from the beach front I decided to circumnavigate the island of so called paradise. All went well until I reached the far side. Rounding the cliffs, they were no longer there to protect me from the ocean's waves. The kayak that was gracefully slicing through still water, now jerked from side to side, righting itself after each wave knocked into it. I struggled with the oar, some of my efforts not even connecting with the water as I was being lifted and dropped as often as the ocean decided. My arms started to hurt. I knew I had to keep paddling or the current would drag me out to sea, next stop the Philippines. As much as I would have liked to visit the country I reckoned this wasn't the best mode of transport to get there.

Head down, focused, fighting. Big efforts made small, gradual progress so the little cliff grew bigger as I neared it. Close to chronic arm cramp, which I've never had before but imagine is quite painful, I finally rounded the cliff and the choppy water became calm – just like that. I stopped paddling and continued panting. The entire population of paradise was on the beach, all six of them enjoying the sun and several cocktails, which even at this distance I could see were red. I took my time paddling to the shore and when I got there I was asked: "What's it like on the other side?"

"Well, it's just as well they built the resort on this side," I said, "or they would have been really taking the piss."

That night I consumed several more cocktails, red as standard, and the conversations flowed, albeit, possibly repeated stories at that. Paradise Island wasn't as expected but then again the expected can be boring and this, it wasn't. I'd return to Hanoi tomorrow and continue south, once again searching for my paradise.

Chapter 4

No money No problems

Hue

The child on the train wouldn't leave me alone. In her youthful innocence, combined with her curiosity, she wondered why I looked different to everyone else in the carriage. She had grown braver, graduating from offering me small pieces of fruit to now using my arm as a pillow, much to the amusement to all those around. Her mother apologised and offered me more fruit. In 20 minutes I'd eaten my daily fruit intake requirement and fell asleep. I dreamed of bananas.

Hue is a smaller, more chilled out version of Hanoi. You can estimate the population of a Vietnamese city by the number of motorbikes crowding the streets. Here I could safely cross a road leisurely and to my delight spotted quite a few rickshaws, for the environmentally-obsessed backpacker. I left my rucksack on the bed of my five dollar a night room, used the bathroom that handily came with it for the same price and left to do a tour like tourists too.

I have always had an interest in the horrific Vietnam war. Being up for the underdog, I'm amazed how the people here first defeated the French and then bewildered the Americans. I've enjoyed all the movies that have been made since and, while in primary school and given the task of 'project of your choice', Vietnam was always mine. Well that and the Titanic, which makes me sound like I have a love for tragic events arising in multiple deaths. I don't. Because of this keen interest I found myself sitting on a bus en route to tour the demilitarised zone (the DMZ). Our tour guide had survived the war. He had been recruited by the Americans as a translator. The bus was mainly made up of Americans and French, curious how their great nations were sent packing or maybe they had heard about the 15 cent beer. Who knows. After an increasingly stifling couple of hours, the bus pulled in at the side of a motorway. Over the constant American-twanged nattering I heard 'Ho Chi Minh Trail' mentioned by the tour guide. I had read about this. The trail had been used to transport weapons and supplies from north to south and became integral in ultimately surviving the years at war. I excitedly left the bus expecting to see a path leading to the trail but a closer listen to the guide confirmed Ho Chi Minh Trail had become Ho Chi Minh highway in recent times. I looked from left to right and felt nothing. Our motorways back home may have taken years to complete and the budget blown within the first few weeks, but the only thing that leaves my mouth open when I see it is the increasing toll charges. I was similarly unimpressed here.

Back on the bus we were treated to some music. The rousing song Khe Sanh by Australian band Cold Chisel, tells the story of a disillusioned Vietnam veteran as he tries to come to terms with life after the war, unable to settle anywhere. We climbed into the hills and disembarked at an old army base. Bunkers, tanks and helicopters were scattered around, now disused but each told a tale of death and destruction. The main enclosure had gone the way of the Ho Chi Minh Trail and had turned into a museum and shop. Distastefully, you were able to purchase old American dog tags since the previous owners weren't around. The bus was filled and we returned to Hue, my head's jukebox broken, the same song lyric on repeat: 'You know the last plane out of Sydney's almost gone.'

Check any Hue guide book for a good place to eat, drink and chill out in the friendliest of atmospheres and Café on Thu Wheels is always up there. I cleverly booked accommodation right opposite so my day started with breakfast there, including a Tiger beer. I'd return for lunch, including a couple more Tiger beers and then dinner which was exclusively Tiger beer.

It was during one of these Tiger-fuelled sessions I met a Tasmanian family. Mel and Malcolm had brought their two children, Oscar and Sam, to Vietnam for two weeks and we all hit it off straight away. Café on Thu Wheels is so called because, apart from providing excellent food and drink, the owner Thu also organises motorbike tours around the city. I assured Thu my motorcycle skills extended further than three days earlier, then proceeded to take off too fast and brake too hard, narrowly missing our three tour guides as they discussed which route to take. After plenty more reassuring was done, we were off, our newly formed biker gang. I soon became aware that on my previous motorbike jaunt, I hadn't encountered much traffic. A motorway-sized roundabout now lay dead ahead. I could see it was already in chaos, without me adding to it. A young man with a 3-seater couch precariously balanced across his motorbike wobbled into view. Another had his family out for the day on his, all five of them. Tonight's dinner of 6 chickens and a pig whizzed by – at least I had a choice I thought. A truck driver, neither speed nor other people seemed to be at the foremost of his mind as he determinedly cut through the surrounding circus acts. My turn. No time to think. I put my head down and ploughed into the ring. My helmet hadn't quite fit properly on my weird-shaped head, they never do, and it slipped to one side. My vision was narrowed by three quarters as the possibility of being hit by a flying chicken quadrupled. I dropped a gear, revved the engine and persuaded my bike to go faster. As quickly as it had come upon me, the single-ringed circus was luckily left in my wake.

Leaving the centre of the city we settled into a nice relaxed single file pace. The busy roads had been replaced by peaceful riverside paths where local fishermen could be observed at work and, when they weren't sleeping, they'd fish some. We continued past small villages with uniformed children to a mountain path and a promised view. At the top we dismounted like cowboy bikers. The Huong River (Perfume River) that cuts Hue in two lay directly below us. On the far side greenery took over where the waterline stopped, and stretched skyward until it was in line with where we stood. A cloudless blue sky had but one imperfection and through that hole shone a blazing sun. No one spoke, we just stared wondering how many miles our gaze took in. Then I noticed something strange, the stage was set but the cast hadn't turned up. The sky was without a single bird. I mentioned this and unusually not one of us could remember seeing a bird since arriving in Vietnam.

The tour concluded without any fatal accidents involving a pig, a couch or me. Myself, Mel and Malcolm returned to our seats in Thu's café and proceeded to drink her entire Tiger beer supply. Like the Irish bar in Hanoi, the walls and ceiling are filled with backpacker scrawls and we added our drunk advice for drunker wannabes before staggering on to the most popular backpacker bar in town, the DMZ. Beered out, cocktails were ordered, re-ordered, invented and re-invented after the ingredients were forgotten. We eventually got on the pool table but had to get off it again to start a game. Mel decided to continuously beat me as the alcohol drained my competitive streak, while Malcolm continuously laughed having apparently never seen his wife beat anyone before. The hours disappeared like minutes on a fast watch and then Malcolm announced they had to go, but first we should arm wrestle – as you do. Malcolm is built like he could play for his national rugby team, whereas I'm built like the guy who controls the remote control car that brings the kicker the cone. But always up for a challenge I began to clear the table of our empty cocktail glasses. Ten minutes later we were locked in battle. To my surprise I wasn't thrown across the room and as stalemate continued I could see Malcolm's face grimace. He let out a groan and the table next to ours started to take notice. We continued out epic meeting of strength and as I started to feel his tree trunk arm give way slightly, the whole bar's attention was on our mismatched pairing. I started to grow in confidence and belief. I could feel the bar will on the underdog. I could feel Malcolm getting tired, I could see his shocked face. The strain reached its summit. With all my strength I pushed down and my worthy opponent's hand touched the table. He immediately jumped back clutching his arm as if an electrical current had just shot through it, shaking it back to life. The bar erupted. We shook hands and as Malcolm turned to leave he gave me a knowing wink, a little too knowing.

It didn't take long before the first challenge came. Having watched me win, every male in the bar now wanted a shot at the title. Still on a high I accepted the first, he wasn't nearly as big as Malcolm – he beat me. Having stupidly accepted a second and third challenge, both of which I lost, my drunk brain cells started working together and I realised what Malcolm had just done. He knew exactly what would happen if the bar saw me beating him. All I could do was laugh and for the rest of the night turn down any other offers to display my so-called strength.

When it was time to leave I left. Like a Vietnamese Carlsberg advert, a string of rickshaws were lined up outside the bar. I chose one and sat into the red cushioned seat. Immediately the driver struck up a conversation. Where was I from? How long had I been travelling for? Did I like the Vietnamese girls? Ireland, two months, yes. He told me he knew a bar where all the Vietnamese girls hang out and he wanted to show me. He said it was near where I was staying so I agreed to go for one drink. I started to get suspicious when he then turned and set off in the opposite direction. We were soon in a part of town I hadn't seen before. As he took a sharp turn off the main street and into an alleyway, I knew this wasn't one of my best decisions. Before I could even think of kicking him off the bike and commandeering the rickshaw illegally, he turned again, this time up a ramp that led straight into a room. I found myself sitting on the back of a rickshaw, in a random room in Vietnam, women on both sides who were now feeling my legs, while my rickshaw driver grinned from ear to ear. My thoughts went from 'how do I get myself into these situations?' to 'how do I get myself out?'.

"Reverse, reverse," I shouted.

All present collapsed into hysterical laughter. My driver turned around and high-fived me, after which each of the girls did the same. I felt like I was part of some strange Vietnamese reality TV show and the joke was on me, whatever it was. Composing himself, my rickshaw driver dropped me home. I don't know why, but I think I made his night.

I met Mel and Malcolm the next morning and we had a good laugh despite debilitating hangovers. They were leaving Hue to continue their holiday but asked me to visit them in Tasmania. How could I refuse? I knew I'd be seeing them again.

*

I was sticking around another day because I had made a promise to my sister. Three years previously she had visited here and befriended a local man, Mr Be. He had become her tour guide, showing her all around the city on the back of his motorbike, even ending up in his house for a spot of karaoke. So armed with a photo she had given me, I walked onto the main street, high noon. This might take awhile I thought. I eye-balled the passing locals, picked a target and pounced.
"Do you know this man?" I asked, trusting the photo forward.
"Of course I do," came the reply, "he's my uncle."

It turned out the first guy I had picked was Mr Be's nephew, Key. Not quite believing my luck, I climbed onto the back of Key's bike and he took me to see Mr Be at his house. I recognised his garden straight away. The tree in the middle was in the photo I now held in my hand. We spent the afternoon drinking coffee and eating bananas. Mr Be, now retired, spoke fondly of my sister and seemed excited telling me where they had visited together. He had plenty of questions to ask about her and answering each one, I missed her even more. I gave Mr Be the photo – my sister, Mr Be and the tree. Then I got my own taken, including the latest addition to the story, Key. I had booked a bus ticket to leave the next day to Hoi An but

I was easily persuaded by Key to cancel the ticket and instead travel on the back of his motorbike. This is exactly what I love about travelling. The unpredictability of it all makes it so hard to plan anything definite. Thanks to a meeting three years ago and a chance meeting today I had been offered the road less travelled.

Hoi An (and the road to)

Key collected me first thing in the morning, took one look at me and suggested our first stop should be a waterfall for a swim. I climbed on the back of the bike wearing my backpack. Key placed my rucksack in front of him, balanced between his legs, while he strained to see over it. Not the safest set-up, but he seemed happy and we were off. We soon broke free of the city's traffic and headed south on the coast road. The open road's freedom cliché had as firm a grip on me now as I had on the bike's saddle. The breeze I felt attempted to cool me as the sun seemed to have plans to melt me to the seat. We turned off the road not long after and bounced from rock to rock on a forested dirt track. When our way turned and dropped I could hear the powerful waterfall momentarily before seeing it, past Key's head and over my rucksack. His foot barely on the brake, I was off the bike and submerged in the cool water. Closing my eyes, I lay back, floating the dead man's way. Hangover headache gone. Body cooled. Refreshed. I was in love with Vietnam.

The plunk of a stone entering the water near me made me open my eyes. A stone's throw away, funnily enough, Key motioned me onto the bike. We were soon back on the coast road, but this time climbing the mountain in our path. If I had foolishly taken the bus I would have been driven straight through the mountain where a tunnel would have halved the journey time.

A formula popped into my head:

Time over possible places you could see multiplied by life being too short = I'd made the right choice.

The view before me was nothing short of immense. As the road twisted its way up the side of the mountain, a stone wall divided the road from the cliff and the blue ocean beyond. We pulled in so we could sit, stare and think. This was the kind of coast road I would have associated with the French Riviera or California, not Vietnam. We continued to climb and at the top I was treated to a bit of history and a piece of lunch. One was a stir-fry, nothing very historic about that, but you never know, maybe I'll research it more. The other were French army bunkers dotted across the mountaintop. Perfectly placed to survey the land below for an oncoming attack or to gather your army buddies together for a photograph.

We started our descent on the far side of the mountain, picking up speed as the road dropped and our weight on the bike pushed it on. The town of Da Nang met us on the valley floor. We were on our final stretch now to Hoi An. My knees were sunburnt, my feet were numb. I was physically tired but excited from what I'd seen and what awaited me. It was evening time when we reached the town. It had taken 6 hours.

The great thing about travelling in Vietnam is backpackers can only go two ways. North to south, as I was doing, or south to north. When the two groups meet great stories are told, advice given, bodily fluids swapped and in some cases extreme U-turns are undertaken for a new travel partner. One of these meetings had placed a business card in my hand for a recommended guesthouse here. It's important to remember that the best advice you'll receive while travelling will come straight from a backpacker's mouth, not your guide book which can't possibly keep up to date.

I entered the hotel's reception area and nearly fell into the swimming pool. For some reason that pool position is quite common here. I paid for a room, put my rucksack to bed since it had had a long day, and headed out. I found a bar with food, drink and a pool table. Three aces for a backpacker. Settling in for the night I got chatting to my fellow reality escapees. An American guy of similar age mentioned his Dad was Vietnamese and he'd always wanted to visit his father's country. He introduced himself, his name was Viet. I suggested he should take a trek up north in Sapa, you never know who you could meet.

Hoi An is famous for its tailors. You can get an excellent tailor-made three- piece suit here for the price of a pair of shoes back home. What's more, they'll keep your measurements on file and a simple call will have your next suit on the next plane. Handy, once you haven't moved onto the next size. Not seeing much need for a suit in my future profession as a professional backpacker, I decided instead on a casual top and shirt. I picked them both out of one of the many catalogues, then picked the colour and material I wanted. After being probed thoroughly with a measuring tape, I was allowed leave the shop and told to return the next day.

I strolled around the town for the day, at this stage used to the Vietnamese way of life. There seemed to be an excitement attached to Hoi An, a feeling that there was always a party taking place or one was going to kick off at any minute and things would get crazy. I went looking for one. The first bar I picked fit the bill as I was engulfed in a sea of people, drinking, dancing, talking, kissing. It was like a casino, but roulette was replaced with fussball and poker with pool tables. Both were surrounded by people, playing and cheering. On the main wall, opposite the bar, a huge mural had been painted. Bono as superman. 'Giving Not Bombing' it read. There's really no escaping him.

The following morning I returned to my tailor to try on my new clothes. After a quick alteration I was all set. The decision had been made the night before to continue on to Nah Trang, where I could learn how to scuba dive, so I returned to Da Nang to catch a train. I sat in the train station, as always it seemed, waiting for my train to come in, and got talking to two Dutch guys. I mentioned I was Irish and they seemed compelled to give me a can of beer. They were travelling in the opposite direction so we swapped stories and advice on where to stay. My train arrived and as I was boarding they placed another can of beer into my hand.

"For the journey," they said, "we love the Irish."

Being Irish really is great I thought, especially when I'm not in Ireland.

Nah Trang

When the Americans finally departed from Vietnam after the war in 1973, they left behind mass destruction and the side effects from Agent Orange that would last for generations. When the French departed someone forgot to pack the recipe for their tasty bread rolls. On the streets of Vietnamese towns all over, mini stalls sell these delicious bread rolls with your choice of topping. I had become a cheese spread and cucumber addict in quick time and no anonymous meeting was going to talk me out of it.

I had left my hotel to sign up for a scuba diving class, starting the next day, when I was distracted by a woman waving a bread roll. She knew an addict when she saw one. The bread crumbs randomly caught in my stubble might have been a give away. A few minutes later, bloated on bread, I found my way to Rainbow Divers, who specialise in diving in rainbow-infested waters I presumed. I was told to report back the next morning at half seven and I started to panic sweat. I hadn't been out of bed that early since I had taken Dublin's dire traffic situation into account to make a lunchtime flight and left the house at

5am. I decided I'd have to go straight to bed to make sure I didn't miss the class. But first, it was time to go out.

A bar, rumoured to be run by the Vietnamese Mafia, I figured was a good place to start. I expected to see small round men who had taken advantage of Hoi An's cheap tailor made suits, smoking cigars while ordering hits – to be played by the DJ of course, but apparently he'd been shot the week before. Instead, the bar had a nightclub-during-the-day feel. A pool table down the back surrounded by Vietnamese girls attracted most of the attention, or did I get that back to front? The girls were very impressive to watch, having mastered the art of laziness and played using just one hand. It may have started because they were afraid of letting their drinks out of sight for fear of being spiked, or to keep their boyfriends under wraps in a roomful of drunk female backpackers. Either way it was a joy to watch and my pool-playing ego took a severe knock.

Early the next morning I fell out of bed, down the stairs, off the curb and through the doors of Rainbow Divers. A pretty impressive fall I thought considering there was a good kilometre from start to finish. There were ten of us in the class and our two instructors talked us through what the following days would entail. It all sounded very exciting until we were told a 200m swim would kick off proceedings. I was a late learner in the swimming department, causing my swimming teacher no end of frustration back when I was 15. When I finally took to it, I was doing 60 lengths every Saturday evening and loved it. A lasting memory of those lessons was of one of the lifeguards leaving to travel Australia. By the time he returned I was just about swimming and he was as tanned as an aborigine. A cool look, I thought, and one I wouldn't mind one day.

I peered into the pool, it looked deep and that was only the shallow end. It stretched 50m from my feet to the far end. I hadn't done this in 15 years but assumed it was like riding a bicycle. Halfway through the first length I realised it was just like that, except the bicycle would be in the water with me and I'd be struggling for breath while trying to change into an easier gear. Through my breath-stained goggles I caught sight of the disappearing pool floor and being in the deep end made me panic. Whatever grace had been in my front stroke vanished as I switched to the doggy paddle of a blind dog with one leg and no ears. Out of breath I scrambled out of the pool having just about done one of the required four lengths.

"That didn't go too bad," I gasped between erratic breaths.

The class was divided in two. I was in the 'not so good' half. In the afternoon we were given scuba equipment. Prior to this, the closest I'd been to scuba was a Bond film, where he seemed to enjoy a night dive in almost all the movies. Suited up, we took to the water again and were taken through the basics, the most important point being 'remember to breathe'.

Having graduated from the swimming pool, the next day we took to the open water. After arriving at the dive site we were paired up with a 'buddy' who we had to swim beside at all times for safety reasons. Holding my mask and mouth piece in place, one giant step off the boat and I was in the water. We descended to the depths down the rope that was attached to the anchor. Every few breaths I had to pop my ears by holding my nose and blowing to release the pressure that was building up. If I didn't keep equalising, the pain was worse than any earache I've had. Reaching the sea bed we grouped together and practised some of the techniques we had learned the day before. I found that once I was doing something, I was fine, but when I was sitting there, waiting on someone else to perfect clearing their mask of water, I could feel the tiniest tingle of panic. It was like the opposite to a fear of heights. Instead of 'don't look down' it was 'don't look up'. 12M underwater, looking through my dive mask, a tunnel of dark water finally reached a glimmer of light as the bright day was alive outside our aquarium. With our oxygen running short we returned to the boat, exhilarated by our first dive and a hunger acquired that would scare a horse.

The next day everybody's confidence was high and we all eagerly stepped off the boat and descended into the warm blue water, this time without the aid of the anchor rope. We paired up with our 'buddies' and set off after our instructor to explore the surrounding sea life. The key to scuba diving, we had learned, is to be very relaxed. Your legs give a slow, deliberate kick while your arms are usually by your side. The less you exert yourself the less oxygen you use up, so the longer you get to enjoy the water world. As we rounded a piece of coral that looked as if it had arrived several thousand years earlier from space, I was slightly behind my buddy. For some reason he picked that very moment to demonstrate he knew the breast stroke. Just before it hit, I saw his hand swing back and make precision contact with my mouth piece, knocking it clear out of my mouth. My air supply had been cut off. We had been shown what to do in a situation like this and practised it in the swimming pool. Importantly you don't panic and with the grace of a mermaid you glance to one side and swing your arm in a slow arch the opposite way, the result being your mouth piece rests safely into your hand. Not surprisingly I thought of none of this. Instead, I invented my own unique mouth piece recovery manoeuvre. With zero grace I flapped and twisted like a rabies infected bat getting down to his local funk cover band, blinding myself in the process with all the bubbles I was creating. Somehow my effort paid off as I felt my life source floating free. I plugged myself back into the mains and started to put together a list of unfortunate names to call my so-called 'buddy'.

Boarding the boat once again I had completed my scuba diving course. The celebrations started back in the diving headquarters, which, handily enough, doubled as a bar, and as the night aged we descended once again, this time on a beach bar called the Sailing Club. The bar is famous for its Jam Jars, a cocktail concoction, strong, but very drinkable, and served in a jam jar. Presumably at some stage, a clean glass in the house could not be found and jam jars took over and caught on. Within no time we were truly jarred. I had forgotten my name and my terrible swimming ability. I ran straight for the ocean. Even this drunk my aim was good and as I crashed into a wave, it crashed into me. The cold water reminded me of my name and of my terrible swimming ability. Before I forgot them again, I found my bed.

We met the following day on the beach, letting the sun melt the previous night's alcohol out of us. I was relaxed, enjoying the good times, maybe this was my paradise. But as the full group reunited on the beach, stories were told. Nah Trang wasn't the safe beachside haven we first thought. After leaving the Sailing Club last night, several of the group were robbed. When a suitable candidate is drunk enough they are descended upon by a large group of Vietnamese women. One of the group was pushed to the ground and they robbed his wallet and shoes. As he angrily but carefully trod home, they reappeared on mopeds and threw his shoes and wallet, minus any cash, back at him. Seemingly, they will always return your pass cards so you can stock up on cash and they can rob you again the next night. How thoughtful of them. Having been robbed several times, an English friend had taken to wearing his money round his neck and had cleverly named the thieves 'Evil Pirate Hookers'. Putting problems aside, we thought with our stomachs and feasted on lobster we bought very cheaply from a local lady on the beach.

The feeling of kings upon us, we visited Nah Trang's very own mud baths. The afternoon was spent covered in mud up to our necks in a selection of different shaped baths. The day was finished with dinner by the pool, the temperature dropped from hot to warm, our mood from happy to happier. Returning to my room later on, my passport whispered the word 'visa' from my bedside locker. I couldn't believe it, my 30-day visa was down to 4, nearly a month had passed and I had never felt it. I checked my email. A friend filled me in on life in the unwanted real world.

"How was your weekend?" she asked.

It made me laugh. I hadn't had a weekend since I left Dublin. The different days existed only as an expanse of time. Honestly, I'd have to think twice as to what month it even was. I'd leave for Ho Chi Minh city tomorrow, my final stop in a country that had me totally absorbed.

Ho Chi Minh

Motorbikes swarmed around my taxi, their combined engines buzzing enough to equally make you take notice of them and drive you mad. My driver had long become immune, as music wasn't even needed to block it out. I peered through the car's side window wishing to see something, anything, that would make me take to this city. I wanted Ho Chi Minh city to contain all the ingredients that had made me love Vietnam so far, but it appeared charmless. Through the traffic I spotted an old woman using the path as a convenient toilet – this place just seemed dirty.

Before I could even step from the taxi into the guest house, I was confronted by a man carrying a huge vertical stack of books.

"You wanna buy book?" he asked.

I was tempted to pick one out quickly from the middle of his pile to see how good he was at juggling, but I resisted and declined. I stepped back onto the street after checking in and was soon set upon by another tourist to tourist book salesman. He was joined by a couple more, making me repeat myself three times. I retreated with my previously purchased book to the very back of a coffee shop. No sooner had I turned a page and taken a sip of coffee, than I was being offered more books. This city was going to take some patience.

While I was in Hanoi I did buy a book off the street. They are a lot cheaper than back home, as expected, but having torn off the cellophane its wrapped in, you realise it's all photocopied. A bit unexpected but too late, as your salesman has vanished.

I had bought a book on the Chu Chi Tunnels that was mostly readable. Halfway through the procedure someone needed to change the toner cartridge in the photocopier and the fading print came alive once again. It was a fantastic read and stories of lives lived out in a complex tunnel system during the war whetted my appetite for the real thing.

The tour I booked left early the next morning. Our bus edged its way through the city and into the countryside. After a couple of hours we stopped for a break at what turned out to be a workshop and gallery. The art of extracting every penny from the tourist was being exhibited. But this was slightly different. The people that work, run and display their art here were all effected by Agent Orange. The Americans dropped over 20 million gallons of this during the war, exposing 4.8 million Vietnamese to it, which resulted in 400,000 deaths and disabilities. Half a million more were born with birth defects. It wasn't nice to see: a slap across the face we all need sometime to remind us we're the lucky ones. We sombrely returned to the bus.

The Chu Chi Tunnels cover a total of 3km and are mainly found under the area known as the Iron Triangle which covers 60 square miles. The Vietnamese mastered the art of surprise during the war, seemingly popping up out of nowhere to dismiss the enemy before disappearing again. The Americans with their Gung Ho attitude and all out blanket bomb style attack, were baffled. When they realised their enemy was living under the very ground they walked on, a new soldier was born. The Tunnel Rat. These fearless humans entered the darkness of tight tunnels, armed only with a handgun, a torch and nerves of unbelievable steel. Often they met their death when they encountered one of the many traps awaiting them. They were considered to be out on their own, a cut above the rest and respected like war heroes. The technical ability of the Vietnamese to build and live in these tunnels was like no other. On one occasion, a tank that the Americans had mislaid, was found by a tunnel rat deep underground. Piece by piece the tank had been dismantled and brought into the tunnels to be rebuilt. The Americans were just astonished. My favourite aside to the war though was how the Vietnamese continued to have as normal a life as possible despite living in a tunnel. Just because a war raged above their heads it didn't mean they should give up on their music and entertainment. At night they'd sneak out of hiding to perform a well-rehearsed play in the open. Huge bomb craters became perfect amphitheatres – built by the Americans, brought to life by the Vietnamese.

We followed a path through the forest, worn by the count-less previous tourists. This had been well bombed and although the wooded area was in full growth again, there seemed to be a relative newness to it. We stopped where an opening in the trees made it possible for us all to stand around our tour guide.

"Where you are standing," he said, "contains an opening to the tunnels, try and find it."

We tried – we couldn't.

He lifted the lid on his well used party piece and revealed a small rectangle in the earth. It seamlessly slotted into the ground like Lego of the same colour. He invited anyone who wanted to, to drop into it, and waistlines were checked. His small frame dropped in, crouched down and replaced the covering. He was gone. The elusive Viet Cong hiding from the bewildered American soldiers.

Continuing on the route, a section had been set up display-ing the most commonly used traps by the Viet Cong. Expertly made, a painful death was assured for anyone unlucky enough to fall foul. Slightly further on, steps down into the dark brought you into another tunnel. It had been adjusted width-wise to ac-commodate the average tourist and to trap and kill the average American I presumed. It stretched 100m in length and we were told every 15m a turn off would lead you out to the open if you felt uncomfortable. This wasn't enough to persuade most of the party of 20, so only 7 of us became tunnel rats. The first thing I noticed was the intense, sticky heat. Lights were dotted irregularly along the roof, releasing a little light to give birth to large shadows. Our adopted hunchback walk soon became redundant as the ceiling dropped us onto our knees in order to keep going. This was already too much for the person in front of me and they pealed off left to daylight. I continued crawling, the red clay embedded onto me, so much so I could taste it. In the dim light from the bulb above my head, I could see the next light was broken. I crawled on and was engulfed in darkness. Pausing, I expected to hear shuffling coming up behind me but my breath was all that broke the silence. The others must have given up too. A ping of doubt entered my head. Had I taken a wrong turn? There wasn't enough room to physically turn around so in my sweat-soaked t-shirt I continued further. I thought about the traps. I thought about a cave-in. I thought about double chocolate fudge cake. I had to get out. I felt my way around another corner, a thin slice of light pinched my view and my way out was ahead. I emerged from a hole in the ground, the full 100m completed and a t-shirt that was now fit for the bin.

Having regained my composure and breath we decamped for some lunch and weapons usage - as they go together. Beside cans of coke and ice creams, a wall display of weapons showed off the available options you could try. Handguns, bazookas and grenades, but a few. Sticking with the Nam theme I decided on an AK47, one of the most used weapons during the war. I ordered an ice cream and some bullets to go. I placed the ill fitting headphones on my head because they wouldn't fit around my waist and shot off a continuous round. My target was an unmissable mound of dirt dead ahead – I missed it twice. I walked away with a buzzing in my ears that would last the rest of the day. Our tour ended with that bang and we were back on the bus to return to the city.

I decided to continue with the current theme and went straight to the war museum. Fighter planes, helicopters and tanks impressively filled the outside area. Inside wasn't a place for the unprepared, and judging by the faces I passed we were all in the same tank. They didn't hold back with their photos, diagrams and memorabilia. This is what happened and this is what they have to live with. Agent Orange. These horrible two words came up again. Photographs of young and old affected by cowardly chemical warfare. I recognised some of the famous images that are flashed around the world whenever talk of the war is brought up. But why, I wondered, had I never seen any of the disturbing Agent Orange photos before? America lost the war but unfortunately won the media war and will remain at the top. They're unable to deny Agent Orange but they certainly aren't going to publicise it. They'll show what they have to and no more. In this media-created world we now live in, I'd love to know what really goes on. I left the museum heavy hearted and full of thought; about what had happened to this most beautiful country, about my previous four weeks. A slogan I noticed when I first arrived and that seemed to follow me since, came to mind. It's simply, 'Same same, but different'. The locals say it, it's printed on t shirts and on posters in bars. When I first heard it, I didn't get it, but after spending 30 days travelling south, I not only understood it but was in love with the very differences Vietnam can boast. This is a country that not 40 years ago was war-torn, meaning the vast majority of people you meet have a direct connection or even fought, and never once did I come across or hear anything close to a grudge being held. The truth is, it's not about the place, it's about the people. They make the country and the people here couldn't be friendlier or happier. Witnessing such a mentality I cringe when I think how often I've heard '800 years' regurgitated back home. We could learn a lot from the Vietnamese. I know I have.

Chapter 5

INTO THE RIVER WE DIVED

Phnom Penh

I woke up and knew I'd slept it out. I had been drinking in a bar opposite my hostel, celebrating my last night in Vietnam. A simple walk across the road would have had me to my bed but I'm not sure I could even find the road at that stage. As if foreseeing this hazy future, I had pre-packed my bags and left them by the door. I got out of bed, conveniently already dressed, grabbed my rucksack and left. The bus was still there but filling up. I loaded my bags and followed my nose.

"Six rolls with cheese spread and cucumber please."

Breakfast, lunch, dinner, hangover cure and addiction fix all in one. Damn, I was going to miss Vietnamese fast food.

Despite only a couple of hours sleep, the closer I got to Cambodia, the less tired I felt. I was getting more and more excited about experiencing a country I'd never been to before. As the hours went by the landscape began to change. I noticed skeletal thin animals at the side of the road and make-shift shacks as houses. This was definitely Vietnam's poorer neighbour. My destination was Cambodia's capital, Phnom Penh, and consulting my guide book it appeared there were two areas that contained backpacker hostels – by the river and by the lake.

Guest house No. 9 by the lake seemed to be the ideal choice for chilling out with other backpackers, so not knowing where the bus had left me, I took a rickshaw there. There, turned out to be just around the corner on a side street that ran parallel to the lake. It looked like it had been copy-and-pasted from Beijing, mixed with Hanoi and Photoshop had taken care of the Cambodian traits. I loved it straight away. My rickshaw driver insisted on coming into the guest house with me and waiting around until I was assured a room. He wanted to show me around his city and said he'd return for me the next day. The owner was a big guy named Kill, possibly suitably named, I didn't want to find out. A mosquito net-covered double bed took up the majority of the room I was shown, leaving a man made partition separating the bathroom. The toilet was move-able and required you to throw a bucket of water down it in order to 'flush'. Still, the bucket was supplied so I was grateful. I took off my rucksack and thanked Kill. He just stood there smiling. I knew they used American dollars here but did they also tip like Americans? If that first moment wasn't awkward, it was now. Kill looked at me and I looked at Kill. Five seconds felt like six as nothing was said. His smile hadn't changed, mine was halfway to Lima.

"You want smoke smoke?" he broke the air with.

Relieved the moment had ended without his name becoming a verb, I thanked him for his kind offer and still not wanting to offend blurted, "maybe later." As I finally closed the door behind him I noticed the rules of the hostel taped to the back. Black bold lettering, top of the list, 'No Drugs'. Obviously Kill had momentarily forgotten his own house rules, possibly due to what he had been smoking.

Guest house No. 9 was like entering rehab. Everything was here for the backpacker who wanted to chill out. DVDs, comfy couches, pool table, music, food, friendly staff and a beautiful lakeside view. Also a bar though, which made it nothing like rehab. It seemed the more people arrived, the earlier we started to drink, and with $4 bottles of Smirnoff the whole ordeal was cheap. To break from the norm of drinking by the bar, during the day we'd take to the lake. Locals in rickety wooden boats would paddle you around the lake for a couple of dollars. Tak-ing a few cans of beer and ignoring the fact that the boat looked like it was going to fall apart, we'd lie back in the afternoon sun, recovering from our hangover by drinking more.

If we weren't on the lake, our favourite way to pass the day was watching any one of the numerous counterfeit DVDs, many of which hadn't yet made the cinema back home. It was while watching one of these I noticed bright flashes of light coming off the lake. I figured a bar further down had a spotlight that randomly roamed the late evening sky to attract attention. The movie ended so I walked out onto the decking that led to the water. I couldn't believe what I saw. A lightning storm was illuminating the lake. Forked lightning would stretch from sky to water and a bright flash would follow to blanket the lake in blue. The eerie thing was, there was total silence. No thunder, no wind, no rain. It was a perfectly still, warm night with electricity in the air. Couches were pulled out, beers ordered, and we watched in awe, not a word spoken. Our digital cameras couldn't capture what was in front of us so we stared, embedding it in our memory.

I had a real problem with the food in Cambodia, nothing appealed to me and I'm not a fussy eater. Maybe it was the month in Vietnam, feasting like a king on the finest food, but now everything tasted dry and stale. As I was playing pool I noticed Richard, one of the staff, cross the floor with what looked like a plate of tasty chocolate pieces. He saw me looking and offered some my way. Contact was made and it was en route to my mouth when he mentioned the word; spider. It took a detour from my mouth and ended up across the bar. Richard laughed and said he had other food I would like instead. I suspiciously followed him to his table and what looked like beef stew was in fact dog, that tasted like bad beef. If there was ever a reason to stick to the drink, I think I found it.

I ran out of excuses to tell my eager rickshaw driver, surely there are only so many days you can be drunk or hungover?! So today, I'd take him up on his offer and see the city. Unfortunately he was nowhere to be found, so quick negotiations were made with another and I was off. I got out at the river. Boats with bars and restaurants gave you the option to walk the plank and board them. The street that ran alongside was a mix of cafés, bars and souvenir shops. Hardly a Cambodian person in sight, this could have been Europe. Around the corner a bustling market reminded you where you were. Stalls tightly crammed in together made it difficult to know if people were haggling for live chickens or replica runners. I walked past a food stand that had as much life on it as the buying public. Crossing the road I entered the calmness of a park and fed an old elephant bananas. Monkeys roamed free, eating whatever scraps of food the tourists left for them and posed for photos.

That night I discovered a bar down the road from the hostel called The Drunken Frog. It was run by Martin from England who was now living here. Soon the whole guest house had filled the rooftop bar, which overlooked the lakeside street. We took turns in picking music and drinks and combined them with new friendships and laughter. It felt like we owned the bar. There was no closing time and no shortage of drink. This was the local I've always wanted, just not conveniently situated from my apartment back home. I thought twice about staying and living a life in Phnom Penh, but my need to know what lay ahead, made me leave. That and the terrible food, because man cannot live on Pimms and coke alone.

Siem Reap

I caught a bus north and over dust and pot holes we travelled to Siem Reap. After the previous night's accommodation I decided on something a little more up scale, or at least with a flushable toilet. Down one of the many side-streets I found both and with a swimming pool thrown in, I took it. Siem Reap was Hanoi to Phnom Penh's Ho Chi Minh. Quaint, laid back and beautiful, it came alive at night. This is a major path crossed by tourists due to the many temples that are found not far from the town. On the street I spotted an Irish rickshaw. Painted green, white and orange with 'Cead mile failte' emblazoned across the back, I had to get in.

"Dia dhuit," I cheekily greeted the Cambodian driver.

"An bhfuil Gaeilge agat?" he replied to my surprise.

"Cupla focail and I've just used them both," I said.

Embarrassingly the conversation stopped dead in its tracks as it soon became clear he had more Irish than myself. I asked to be brought to Angkor Wat and avoided questions as to why I didn't speak my own language along the way. Angkor Wat (meaning temple) was created in the 12th century and is the largest and most visited of the five temples in Siem Reap's surrounding area. It didn't take long to get there and my driver said he'd stick around to bring me back to the town afterwards. After spending the afternoon walking I figured this was a good time for a massage.

One of the many flyers I had been handed earlier suggested a four-hand massage for $10. I thought this was a good suggestion. It was the kind of place that would take your coat when you entered, except it was over 30 degrees outside so I didn't have one. Instead my hand was taken as I was led into the back and handed a pair of brown pyjamas. Looking the part of an 80-year-old I was ushered through curtains and onto a mattressed floor. Two Cambodian girls arrived, dismissing images I had of a 4-handed mutant masseuse who was just learning her trade. Luckily the girls knew what to do and in no time one was sitting on my back while massaging my legs while the other sat on her shoulders and massaged my ears. Things started to get a little strange after a change of position and I found myself massaging an elbow while someone stood on my neck, but soon my feet were untied and we were back on track. In 60 minutes the hour was up and I was sipping on a herbal tea, while the girls dragged hard on their cigarettes. I think it was as good for them too.

When it was time for dinner I longed for something I could eat. I found an unsuitably sounding restaurant called The Dead Fish, and holding my nose I walked inside. The structure of the place was delightfully dangerous, like an unfinished attic, but it had charm. Unprotected wooden stairs led to different levels where, still unprotected, you sat on the floor and ate from a ground level table. If you lent back or stumbled, you were over the side. I rated each level by the injury you might receive if you fell. The 'broken arm' level was taken by sensible locals. There seemed to be room in the higher up 'broken leg' area, which I asked for. Further up still, the 'broken neck' area seemed to be under a state of repair, although it was hard to say when you considered the place as a whole, and at the top, the 'certain death' area was full with party-hard Chinese. Amazingly, they seemed to be drinking by the shot and at the rate they were going it was probably going to be safer for them to spend the night up there. I did mention the place had charm though, didn't I? Well, under certain open-sided walkways, a crocodile pit lay. Broken neck or arms aside, the crocodile wouldn't mind, he'd eat all three.

I declined a drink, ordered fish and chips, and it was the first meal in Cambodia I really enjoyed, but I didn't finish. All through dinner I kept my gaze on the walkway, wondering would the crocodiles be fed tonight, but wisely the Chinese had stayed put. So wanting to see some croc action before I left, I fed them my leftovers. They fought over a couple of chips I threw in, although there was no need because there was one for each of them, and then they politely divided my fish. I left for my bed, wondering how the Chinese would sleep up there in their tree house.

I got up early, just after lunch, and decided it was time to log on to the real world, but just for a short time in case I got trapped. A man sat down at the computer next to me and I noticed his Dublin jersey straight away. Another glance and I noticed he was Asian or from the northside somewhere, it was difficult to say.

"You support the Dubs?" I offered.

"I prefer my home county," he replied in a thick Navan accent.

He saw my amused look and explained back in the day, when Albert Reynolds was handing out passports like sweets, he got

one. He set up a business in Navan and has lived there ever since. He was over in Cambodia on holiday visiting his sister.
"So you're not from the northside then?"

After practising my floating in the pool for the afternoon, I had a look at the map of the town. Bar Street for some reason caught my eye. I hadn't a notion what delights might await me there but I felt I had to find out. As it transpired, Bar Street is like a mini Khao San road, more of which when I get there. Bars, nightclubs and restaurants populate a pedestrianised stretch of road about 200m long. People fill the bars and spill out onto the road, trying not to spill their precious drinks in doing so. I opted for a small corner restaurant that had an open air rooftop dining area with a view of the whole street below. After eating my fill, I drank it too with cocktails and handed my waitress a $20 note. She returned to my table with the manager and a look of regret.

"We can't take this money," she said, "it has a hole in it."

Taken aback, I took it back expecting my finger to go straight through it.

I couldn't see any hole though and seeing my confused look, she pointed it out. Near the top right corner, no bigger then a pin hole, and holding it up to the light to see it, was the offending hole that deemed my currency void.

I exchanged it for another, which they both examined thoroughly before thanking me. They'd probably go into shock if they worked in Dublin, seeing our often ripped and cellotaped cash.

I left the restaurant, fought my way through the packed street and into one of the busy bars. The only gaps between people were caused by several pool tables, used for both sitting and playing. In the bar's bedlam I managed to exchange my dodgy currency for several cocktails and a promised headache. Most of the other backpackers from Guest House No.9 had arrived in Siem Reap so we continued where we had left off. We found a bar that didn't close, music that didn't stop and a cocktail they didn't sell anywhere else. They each played their part until the rising sun hurt our eyes and with sore heads we found bed.

From the moment I first arrived in Asia there was one word I heard repeatedly. Tubing. Everyone who had done it, raved about it, and it seemed anyone who hadn't, was on their way to do it. After sleep, I would continue north to Laos, and find out what all the talk was about.

Laos

I joined the queue at the border, waiting for my turn to have my visa issued and passport stamped. My passport was starting to fill up. Entry and exit stamps to the countries I'd visited, gave the dates but revealed little else. A diary that confirmed I had simply been there at a certain time.

My passport was handed back to me with confirmation that I existed right now and in this exact place, which was nice to know. A short drive in a Tuk Tuk brought me into Laos' capital, Vientiane. This didn't read well in the guide book. It seemed to be only mentioned as a place to get from A to B, B being in this case, home of tubing, Vang Vieng. I checked into a guest house and paid also for a bus, leaving the next morning. En route to dinner and drinks I stopped at a pass machine to extract some local currency. My credit card was rejected. Not due to the lack of funds, not yet anyway, but because the ATM machines here only accepted mastercard. Luckily I had American dollars tucked away for emergencies, as all Asian countries accept both their currency and the dollar.

That night I ate in a local bar. This was a place as modern as you'd find on Dublin's Grafton Street. The circular outdoor bar had a TV pointing at you no matter where you sat, forcing you to watch the pub's best friend, sport by satellite. Inside, a more formal dining area was full of people flickering in candle light as a band in the corner were setting up for the night ahead. The food was European, leaving my pallet as confused as the rest of me as to what country I was in. I returned to my Laos bed and dreamed of things American.

I was on a bus by ten the next morning, again heading north, this time to Vang Vieng. Once the city was dispersed of, thick jungle took over either side of the bus. Greens faded into other greens and to count the different shades would have been impossible. We stopped halfway at a purpose-built shop and gathered together under the shade of a tree to eat ice creams. Our bus didn't have air con but we'd been lucky so far, it was still running. I had heard the buses here had a bad habit of breaking down frequently. We lasted another three hours on the bus, the bus lasting another three on the road, before pulling into a small car park, our destination reached. If it had been a cartoon all four wheels would have then fallen off spontaneously, but instead the driver patted the bonnet and whispered congratulatory words to the engine. Guest house owners were out in numbers to try and entice you back to theirs. I chose Mom's Guest House, but the dream of home cooked meals was short lived.

Vang Vieng is a small and very beautifully picturesque town. The main street, containing plenty of bars and restaurants, leads to the Mekong River where impressive cliffs dwarf both. This is tubing central, the reason we're all here. As I made the short walk into the town I passed a bar called 'Jack Johnson'. Maybe it had the same owner as Paradise Island. An owner with impeccably bad taste in music and in this case, someone who was placing the success of his business on the popularity of a tiresome singer songwriter. To say the place was empty though would be a lie. The staff were there.

The bars here are taken advantage of on the days you're not tubing, each one set up for relaxation. Large TVs are used to watch any of the huge selection of DVDs while lying back on a couch bed, submerged in cushions. Repeated re-runs of Friends aren't uncommon, as you drift in and out of sleep. That night I crossed the Mekong River on a bamboo made bridge. The far side is known as the Island. I followed a path through long grass and trees until the flames of a fire danced the dark to light. A wooden hut revealed a bar where drinks were served by the bucket. Small wooden square piers had been built, dotted alongside the river, resembling booths in a bar. After choosing one, cushions and candles were sent over and vodka buckets were drunk. The night, like life, stretched before us, but in our booth bubble, laughter seemed to make it all stand still. Irish, English, Scottish and Dutch came together that night and solved the world's problems. Great minds, avoiding reality but living life. The next day we'd sit in large inflated tires and float down a river.

Between us we decided to pay the $2 extra to get a tour guide, which really meant that for $7 each we rented the tubes and a guy in a canoe to look after our valuables while we drank and swam. We hopped into a minivan after loading our tubes onto the roof and drove 10km out of town. The tubing idea is very simple. You rent a big inflatable tyre that you sit in and float peacefully downstream for the day, back to Vang Vieng. Throw in a few bars and swings, and peaceful becomes exciting.

The day was perfect. The cliffs that climbed out of the water to our right reached a cloudless blue sky that hugged the heat-giving sun. We paddled with our arms, the lukewarm water contrasting with the sun's rays to produce the right temperature. We floated with a slow ease that now became life's perfect pace. We lay back, we closed our eyes, we splashed water, we laughed, we held hands. Even the most uptight person would drift to carefree as the water carried you where you felt, right now, you were meant to be.

The first 5km played out this way until a bend in the river was passed and the low thud of a beat skipped across the water to our ears. Up ahead was the first of the bars we'd meet and the beginning of our drinking day, it was just after 11. As we approached, ropes were thrown out to us and we were pulled in to the shore. We parked our tubes and ordered drinks, by the bucket, of course. Each bar had its own swing that would fling you out to the middle of the deep river. Before the current took you, you had to swim back to the bar. We all took turns, celebrating surviving with a local shot called Laos Laos that tasted and looked like mud water.

We finished our drinks, re-launched our tubes and merrily continued further downstream to the next bar. Soon the bar's swing was in sight, as we watched people somersaulting into the water. This, we found out, was the main bar. It had the biggest swing and football tennis and volleyball courts. The Killers blared from the many speakers as we clambered ashore, assured it was only a kiss. Our tour guide fished out everybody's money from his waterproof bag and soon buckets were once again in hand. We joined in with the ongoing games. People continuously left and arrived, the games never ended, the scores uncounted. I then joined the queue for the swing, climbed the horizontal wooden planks that had been nailed to the tree and reached the top to take my turn. Slightly further up the tree a local man pulled the swing back in after each go. I stood on the V shaped planks, took hold of the swing and as an aside, asked how safe it was. He just laughed. I could feel the alcohol mix with my nervous excitement. I pushed off, raced through the air and took momentary flight before crashing into the water. I swam back to the shore, buzzed and ready for another drink.

After awhile our tour guide rounded us up. He explained how it would get dark by half five and importantly there was another bar to visit. We were off again, this time in full voice floating side by side down the river – "Cause I'm Mr. Brightside." At the final bar a bonfire had been lit. We ordered more drink and warmed ourselves off the fire's flames while Bob Dylan announced the times are a changin'. There was one more swing to do so we took turns to leave the fire's warmth and get wet again. As it was also the last swing of the day it was suggested we'd team up and do the swing as a doubles team. So myself and my English friend, Kia, side by side, counted down and let the swing adhere to gravity. We both dropped into the middle of the river and emerged from the water, one after the other. I was still slightly out of breath from the previous attempts, so I put my head down and swam back to where I could stand in the water. I thought Kia was behind me but when I turned I couldn't see her. I shouted up to the onlookers at the bar and they pointed further downstream. Something was wrong. Although a far better swimmer than me, she was struggling in the water and the current was carrying her further from safety.

Remembering my 'Baywatch' watching days and ignoring the fact that my own swimming wasn't up to scratch, I jumped back in. The current assisted me and I was soon beside her. Dropping from the swing she had hit the water and winded herself. Unable to catch her breath, she was in a panic, struggling to stay above the waterline, and on seeing her rescuer now, it did nothing to calm her. I put my arm around her and tilted her head back, then I tried for the shore. Pretty soon I realised we were both in trouble, a fact I'm sure she already knew, as the current continued to take us downstream. I had read about tubing in my guide book before I arrived. A paragraph now returned to my thoughts. Five people had died in the previous two years. As much fun as it is, alcohol and water don't mix very well when you drink one and submerse yourself in the other. But this wasn't where my trip was going to end. I told her to calm down and kick her legs with me. I used my free arm to push through the water. Slowly we made progress and relief finally swept through me as I touched the riverbed. I was completely out of breath. We sat there, just the two of us, realising that if you get in trouble out here, only your friends will help you. She broke down in tears, terrified, relieved, emotional. I needed a drink.

It was dark when we left the bar. Sitting back in our tubes the water now sent a chill up our backs. Afraid of going missing in the darkness we all linked arms and floated back towards Vang

Vieng. Then somewhere up ahead we could hear a song, "Oró sé do bheatha bhaile." We called out, "Marco." The reply came, "Polo." We floated closer and discovered a group of Irish lads who were not quite sure where they were. We joined together, cold, drunk, tired and sang our way home. As we approached the town, a group of kids appeared, offering to help the weary travellers with their tubes. On the shore, a couple in their 60s stood. She wasn't happy. He had just had one of his best days, resulting in him unable to make his way up a small incline. We linked arms once again and together walked into town, knowing days didn't come much better than this.

I now knew what tubing was all about and understood its 'must do' popularity. But I had to keep going and see what else was out there. I paid for a bus to Bangkok and was told it would take 24 hours. After a short stop over in Vientiane I was on the road south, leaving Laos behind and entering Thailand.

Chapter 6

PARADISE FOUND

Bangkok

The scenery changed, the roads improved and sightings of the King hit double figures. I don't mean Elvis, he has long since left the planet shortly after he left the building, I mean the King of Thailand. Worshipped and adored by the people here, his picture appears on the motorway as often as the maximum speed limit signs. The last thing you want to do is offend him. That, or get caught smuggling drugs, will most likely land you in the famous Bangkok Hilton. Unlike other Hiltons, room service is not an option and you don't have to worry about vacating your room before 12 since you're most likely there for several lifetimes.

The bus let me out at Khao San Road where I was immediately taken in by the sights, sounds and smells. This neon nest is like the backpacker's base camp. A mass of international travellers starting, in the middle of, or ending their trip, but all here for one solitary reason - to party. Alex Garland wrote about it in his book, The Beach. How its very being can stick to you and get under your skin, but even the resulting movie wasn't enough to put people off. Bangkok is on most gap-year maps and Khao San Road is its heart. In our latest crazed poker age, knowing when to fold here is important. I now spotted Elvis. He had arrived here on his own gap year a long time ago and got sucked into its way of life. He had found his plastic girl and they shared a dream of escape both thinking Khao San had the answer. Wrinkles and years rolled on and they were still living out of a rucksack at the Heartbreak Hostel.

I decided to stay across the road on Rambuttri. Only a two-minute walk from Khao San, you could retreat from the madness when you needed to. Rambuttri has its own charm. Lined with guest houses, clothes shops and street stalls, selling food, books and music. Bars advertised on chalk boards the list of movies they'd be showing that day, a 'Beach' marathon wasn't unusual. A Volkswagen van parked at the side of the road transformed into a bar at night. Its side dropped to become a counter and barstools appeared. The boot opened to reveal decks and the barman doubled as a DJ. I continued walking, picked a guest house at the far end, settled in and changed for the night.

It was my friend's birthday back home so I made a phone call. Modern technology connected us as if we were side by side but our worlds couldn't have been further apart. I checked my email. A work question awaited from the person who had taken over my position. Before leaving I assured him it was fine to email me any queries, I didn't mind helping out. I stared blankly at the screen. I had no idea of the answer. The question wasn't difficult, it just didn't fit into this world. It may as well have arrived from space and been in a different language. I walked on to Khao San to find people I understood.

Not much had changed since the daylight disappeared; the street was still awash with life. Street bars sparred over the cheapest drink and the loudest music but shared the tables and chairs. Travellers toasted with buckets and sealed travel plans with kisses. A large group of lady boys sat sipping cocktails. I'd heard all the stories. Most of them had invested time, money and style to look as convincing as they did. Others, the 'lazy boys' we'll say, were simply men in dresses. Still, if there was any place on Earth they could get lucky, I'm sure it was here. I ordered a cheap bucket, which also claimed to be the strongest on the street, and joined the people who understood me.

As the drinks were drunk we soon realised the one thing the street bars were missing – a toilet. Different establishments' bathrooms were used, including the local police station's. With Dutch curiosity, Bangkok's famous ping pong show was suggested. We crammed into a couple of Tuk Tuks and they had us on our way. Just like the movies, a suitably dark alleyway was found, with a single door that opened to a long corridor, a stairs, a dangerous looking bouncer, but then the surprise – a theatre. We took our seats among the other travellers who had found themselves there and also wondered why. Over the next half hour a mixture of women displayed a variety of skills they had somehow possessed that involved ping pong balls and them being bottomless. With scary speed and accuracy, ping pong balls hit far off targets and burst inflated balloons held by the audience. Bottles of coke were opened and candles blown out. As good looking as they were, everybody was terrified of these women. We shuffled out, watching our backs, ignoring the kids selling coke.

The night was old but the morning was young so we found a nightclub. A mirrored dance floor was matched with a mirrored ceiling and with the added drink I thought I was dancing upside down. I changed moves and thought I was back to front. When I then thought I might even be inside out it was time all three of me left the dance floor. I found the toilet and ventured inside, eager to go. As we're so used to now, a toilet assistant was already there. I've been toilet trained since I was two and part of that training involved washing and drying my own hands. I'm pleased to say I still do it myself these days but I'm forever finding myself handing over money for no reason. I gave him a nod and stood at the urinal. Before I could produce the first drop he had placed a wet warm towel around my neck. It was surprisingly soothing and would have relaxed me even more only I noticed he was still hovering behind me. Still dropless, now I suddenly felt his hands on my shoulders as he removed the towel and started to massage me. I was lost for words and the urgent need to urinate. My protest came too late, his hands grasped my neck and with a sudden movement he had cracked it like a large knuckle. I let out an exasperated breath and nervous laugh. As weird as the situation was, my neck felt great. Not waiting around, he twisted my neck in the opposite direction to considerable more cracking. I no longer needed to go to the toilet. I zipped back up and turned to face him, a wide smile on his face. I handed over a few dollars and remembered what a wise man once said. 'Why urinal, when you can cubicle?" I bet he never had a massage in a Bangkok toilet though.

After my first night out in Bangkok I woke up late, I little too late I thought when I noticed it was dark again. I decided to cut my losses, go back to sleep, and than get up early.

Feeling surprisingly refreshed, the sun welcomed me as I dropped my sun glasses on to my nose and walked out to greet it. A stall I hadn't noticed the previous day was selling freshly squeezed orange juice in plastic bottles. I was handed one from an ice cooler and at first sip it surpassed any juice I've ever tasted before. Maybe I was tasting the sunshine or the healthy vitamin C but I knew I had discovered a hangover cure in a bottle. With a mouthful of orange bits I returned to Khao San. The bar I'd sat at the night before, on a bucket binge, had now been replaced with stalls selling music and movies. For as little as 50 cent, albums could be bought and uploaded to your MP3. I looked through the catalogue of artists, picked out a few that I wanted and the guy went to work on his laptop.

After travelling for some time you miss the simple pleasures you had on your doorstep back home. Often, you find you don't take advantage of them because you know they'll always be there, but once you take them away, you wish you had. This had brought a few of us to one of Bangkok's large shopping centres. It wasn't joining a large queue for groceries we missed, it was the cinema. We weren't there to see any particular film, we just wanted the movie-going experience again. Giddy like children, we bought coke and popcorn and relaxed into the soft cushioned seats. The lights dimmed, the curtains drew back, digital life was borne onto the large screen. Everyone in the cinema then stood up. We looked at each other, confused. A slide show of photos appeared on the screen. Soundtracked to orchestrated music, the king was depicted writing, helping a small child and pointing. Propaganda hadn't been so cheesy since the '80s. After the movie we wondered if there was anything else that would give us a Western fix, so we looked around. Excitedly, a bowling alley was found next to a hardware outlet, so we clambered in for a few games and after, walked away with free socks.

Opposite my guest house I had noticed a sign offering different types of massages, one of which was Swedish. I'd never had one of those before but imagined a very apt blonde had been flown from Stockholm to help out weary backpackers, and if she had come all this way, I figured it would be rude not to let her place her hands all over me. A very Thai-looking Swedish girl brought me into a long room. So Thai-looking in fact, she wasn't Swedish at all. I twigged this when she had no idea where her massage technique originated from. There was another guy at the end of the room, enjoying a relaxing massage, at least I thought he was until he loudly declared he'd had enough and bolted towards the door. My masseuse laughed and rolled me onto my front. Without warning an elbow and knee were strongly prodded into my back. Then, as if this wasn't sore enough, my arms were pulled backwards, forcing the knee harder against my skin. My face contorted in pain, hoping the pleasure would start soon. I understood the other guy now and how right he was. The pleasure came when the massage finally came to an end, and I rolled up into a ball, sucking my thumb. Walking with a limp and having developed a twitch, I booked a bus north to Chang Mai.

Chang Mai

It took 12 hours to get to Chang Mai from Bangkok by bus, so, to save on a guest house, I travelled through the night. A beautiful morning woke me as we arrived into the town, the sun heating up the window my head leaned on. There was a medieval feel to the town with its surrounding river and wooden walkway bridges. I paid $5 for a room with a fan, declining the option of air con for a further $2. I was getting used to Asia's heat at this stage. Just like Sapa I had come here to trek. In Bangkok I was given a recommendation and a business card. TIC Travel specialised in one or three-day treks in the jungle and not relocating tiny insects as the name suggests, although you might be unfortunate to do so unknowingly. I walked into a friendly atmosphere, all smiles and handshakes and I signed up for a three-day trek leaving the next day after they had talked themselves up so much I imagined Everest wouldn't have been a problem. I paid in full and filled out a detailed form, which included my passport and room number. They promised to collect me the following morning and with a warm feeling I returned to my guest house where I ate and rested up in anticipation.

The day started early and with a Mexican wave of handshakes I was introduced to the rest of the trekking party where we were now all seated in the back of a truck. Within a couple of hours we were deep in the jungle. Mr. T would be our tour guide for the coming three days, taking care of our party of 12. We were eased into our first day of walking, with each of us getting an elephant. I climbed atop mine, feeling like Tarzan who wouldn't mind feeling Jane. I christened her Dumbo as she insistently flapped her ears as if trying to take off in flight. She was heavily pregnant but seemed to have no issues with the irregular terrain. By the time we'd discussed her maternity leave, whether she was going to return to work after and the extortionate price of crèches, it was lunch.

As well as being our tour guide, Mr. T was also our resident cook. In 20 minutes we had more rice than you could count in front of us, which was really just a bowl each, but mixed with vegetables it filled us up. The hard work followed, as from our table, the rest of the day would be spent walking at an upwards angle. The sun might only have glimpsed us in between our tree cover but the heat was all around. I sweated out any alcohol that remained in my system and ached from every muscle that isn't used in lifting a pint glass. We rested only to let the worse off catch up and continued to climb the mountain. My t-shirt was sweat-covered and my backpack pinned it uncomfortably against my skin, but I was enjoying myself, loving the physical challenge. As the evening brought a haze over the valley floor that announced the sun's surrender for the day, we walked into the mountaintop village.

A raised three-room house was our shelter for the night, a room to cook, one to eat and the other to sleep. The view from the wooden balcony took in the rest of the village and in the background the mountain walk we had conquered disappeared into the valley. A small outhouse was divided into three cubicles, a hole in the ground of each – the toilets. There was no electricity and knowing one of these cubicles in the dark would be even less homely, we used the remaining daylight taking turns braving nature's call. Dinner was soon ready so we all sat around a small fire in the centre of the now smoke-filled room. More rice was dished out, this time accompanied by cooked pumpkin. Starving after the day's hard work, we greedily tucked in.

Having eaten our fill, we sat back, listening to stories, which I suspect were thought up purely for tourist entertainment. I felt a stab of pain in my stomach, put my beer down and switched to water. The cheap bottled water tasted more like a heavy chlorinated swimming pool. I wasn't alone in discomfort though as either side of me the experience was being had and glances exchanged. I was first to make a move, darting from the house the 30m to the now dark toilets. I vomited loudly down the hole, the awful taste of pumpkin back in my mouth, my nose unhappy with the smell. I then changed positions to use the toilet as normal, whatever was inside me wanted out, fast. In my 30 years of residency on planet Earth I have never been so sick. When I returned to the house sleep had taken most of the rest. I knew I wasn't going to be sleeping that night so I lay on the wooden floor, alone, waiting on the stomach cramps to build up to the unbearable again, forcing me out into the darkness. The local dogs were even avoiding me now. As the hours slowly went by, my lonely pilgrimage continued, but my strength was fading. I could no longer make the short walk away from the house so I sat on the bottom step. Alert only to vomit, and asleep for the short time the stomach cramps subsided. My head hung low as colour crept into the once dark clouds. I had nothing left inside, my throat was sore from retching.

With the dawn arrived Mr. T. I could have done with the A Team showing up and air lifting me home in a bamboo-made helicopter, all the time pitying the fool in the back, but unfortunately I had to make do with the tour guide. His genius suggestion was two cups of herbal tea that was more leaf than hot water. I told him my trek was over and the little energy I had would have to get me back to the guest house. Two others who were feeling similar effects of the previous night's dinner, opted to do the same. Motorbikes arrived to take us down the mountain and a truck from there back to Chang Mai. I collapsed onto my guest house bed and fell in love with the idea of en suite bathrooms.

I woke up the next morning with the hunger of a cured sick person. Before I started to eat the mattress I got up and ordered everything I recognised from the menu, which turned out to be just toast, but plenty of it. I decided to take a trip back to TIC Travel, not to complain, as I was more than entitled to do, but to get a refund, as I had only done the one-day trek instead of the three. They had been so friendly when I booked it, I didn't think I'd have a problem.

When I arrived I sensed a different atmosphere. The smiles and handshakes that made up the friendly nature were gone. I politely explained my situation and it was ignorantly discarded. I strongly pointed out that their tour guide had given me food poisoning, but this was met with demands to see a doctor's report. I figured the only doctor I would have gotten atop the mountain would have been a witch doctor and I don't think they write prescriptions or pay tax, let alone write reports. But stubborn as Dublin traffic I refused to leave, principle over money now and still we argued. Finally, just to get rid of me they said, a partial refund was agreed on. As the cash was being handed over Mr. T walked in. After realising I was being refunded he went into a rage his namesake is better known for. I shook it off and left. I hadn't gone too far though when Mr. T and his friend passed me on a moped. They pulled in up ahead and got off the bike. Slightly confused I kept walking until I saw the internationally known 'I'm going to kick the shit out of you' signal – they pushed their sleeves up past their elbows. I couldn't believe it. This was a busy street with a police station on the far side, and these guys had only one thing on their small minds. But this was Thailand, home of Thai boxing, a sport that didn't seem too concerned with rules. So I hopped in a Tuk Tuk and went go-karting with my refunded money.

I was chuffed after I recorded the fastest lap of the day, ultimately setting myself up to take first place. It would have been even better if I had   anyone to compete against, but the day's earlier argument had been forgotten by the time I rounded my last corner, so all was good. I Tuk Tuked back to town and strolled happily through the streets in the direction of the guest house. The annoying sound of a moped interrupted my thoughts and then Mr. T's voice interrupted my happiness. He was alone this time.

"Where were you for the last two hours?" he barked.

"Why?" I replied.

"My gang have been looking for you, you're a bad tourist, never come back to Thailand," he shouted.

"What?" I managed, "Your gang?"

What the hell was wrong with this guy?

He took out his mobile phone and tried to make a call. Bad reception or the lack of credit was on my side.

Frustrated he said, "Wait here," before shooting off.

I politely hung around for half an hour. Well, not really. When an apparent psychotic Thai boxer with a personality disorder asks you to stay – you go. I returned to my guest house and tried not to think of the form I'd filled out in TIC Travel which included my guest house room number. My bus was returning me to Bangkok in the morning where I'd continue south, a choice of islands to choose from. I slept fitfully throughout the night and dreamt of caramel squares.

En route to the islands

Another night in Bangkok was washed down with a few cocktails. I thought about staying but my flight check-in time saw to it that I left. My travel companion now was a Swedish girl I met in Beijing. I turned down the offer of a massage before it was offered. Through the plane's porthole the late afternoon sun danced on her soft golden blonde hair but her hand was tense in mine, she didn't like flying. A 30-minute wait on the plane to be told we'd have to disembark due to faulty air con didn't help. Back in the terminal we waited in silence. Reassured the plane was now fine, I reassured her as best I could and soon we were above the clouds. The short flight landed us in Krabi. We had decided to travel to the islands off Thailand's west coast as opposed to the more popular Koh Phangan east side. The morning would see us leave Krabi by boat.

We walked the streets in search of accommodation but everyone that came from the airport had the same idea. Our rucksacks seemed to get heavier with each 'sorry, we're full' we heard. With our energy fading we found refuge, a shower and an Irish bar's stew. The clink of glasses soon signalled lights out and eyes shut.

The weather had changed and it was under a dull overcast sky we loaded our bags onto a small wooden boat. Eight people on board filled it to capacity. With no sail to set, the engine was switched on and for the next couple of hours we hugged the coastline, out along the peninsula to Riley.

The boat left us as near to the beach as it could and then it was our turn to paddle the remainder of the way. Riley has two beaches, one either side of the peninsula. We landed on the backpacker side, lined with cheap bars and budget accommodation, but a not so nice beach. A short walk to the far side became five star. Posh hotels with private villas, restaurants, bars and pools lined a spectacular beach. Cliffs enclosed it either side where rock-climbers could be seen getting closer to the sun. This was far beyond my budget but the beautiful beach was free so the daytime could be spent in five-star surroundings before retreating with the other budget-tied travellers to our slightly down-market residence.

My accommodation blended in perfectly with the surrounding undergrowth. Across from my wooden room more trees were being cut down to be used to build several more rooms. A large wooden bar and restaurant was situated by the reception area, looking out onto the water we paddled in through. Evening meals made you forget which side of the peninsula you were staying though. Anyone staying here was treated to a seafood barbecue. Barracuda, Shark and my new favourite, Marlin. Seconds would have been had but they soon ran out of food. With our stomachs full, card games were about all we could manage until tiredness caught up on us. I retreated to my tree house bedroom, and to blend in, slept like a log.

Phi Phi

After relaxing for a couple of days, the early rise to catch a boat to Phi Phi Island shouldn't have been a problem, but it was – I hate early mornings. A large crowd assembled on the beach, the rucksacks alone dropping the stars from five to three. We piled onto the boat, each one of us hoping for a seat and the chance of more sleep. Right on cue the clouds that hung around the previous days, departed as we neared Phi Phi. The sea became a lighter shade of blue and we could see the fish play over the side of the boat. By the time we reached the pier, the pieces of my paradise puzzle were filling up. The blue sky reflected in the clear water as the sun heated the white sand of the beach my gaze was now fixed upon. In a perfect arc it drew further from my sight. Palm trees seemed to effortlessly meet perfect geometric standards as they followed the sand yonder. A welcoming committee of a shoal of fish swam alongside the pier. I could make out each one perfectly. If I ever became a fish, these are the waters I'd want to swim in.

Like an airport arrivals lounge, the pier was lined with people holding A4 signs. Fancy-sounding hotel names paired with lucky arrivals. I spotted five stars but didn't think I could pass as a Sinead Kelly, so continued on to the conveniently located travel agent. It didn't take long to source the cheapest room on the island and only a ten-minute walk from the pier. As I made my way through the tiny streets, busy with buyers and sellers, I noticed how clean and new everything was. This was the result of the tsunami that destroyed the island on St Stephen's Day 2004. That day, as holidaymakers lay on the beach enjoying the Christmas sun, the tide went out all of a sudden. The more curious started to follow it. The horror that must have been felt when they realised what was going to happen is unimaginable. Today's Phi Phi is a changed place with a new understanding of how fragile life can be. Plaques hang in bars remembering friends and workmates lost. Unfortunate enough to be down to work that day, never to clock out. Advancing further on towards my accommodation, newly-erected tsunami signs pointed the way to safety if it were to happen again. They were all pointed in the direction I was staying, a nice peace of mind I thought. My room had everything that I needed – in total, a bed. But closer inspection of it would have to wait. I changed and headed to the beach.

I took my shades off, making sure they weren't somehow enhancing what I was seeing as I stepped onto the sandy curved beach. Sun worshippers stretched its length in both directions. Music floated from a central beach bar where beers and backgammon were enjoyed. I walked out into the ocean and sat down and lay back and closed my eyes. The warm water lapped against my ears, in and out. I thought about paradise. I thought about Phi Phi. I thought about how they had more in common than starting with the same letter. Then I was hungry so it was time to eat.

I wandered back onto the streets, passing building work that was still in progress. They had managed to do a remarkable job in three years. Luckily the tsunami threat to Dublin is non-existent, but if our light rail development is anything to go by, the rebuilding of the city would take several consecutive lifetimes of healthy old aged men and cost the world – would it really be worth it? Well, Phi Phi certainly was. The afternoon was spent in a secondhand book shop that served great coffee; an Irish bar loomed large opposite me.

Through the magic of Facebook I met up with people I'd run into in the previous weeks. Acting like a global GPS system it can amazingly find people anywhere in the world – as long as they say where they are and, of course, how they feel, just in case you wanted to know. Like all good reunion parties that I've been to, stories were swopped, laughs were had and copious amounts of drink were drunk in the moments faces were far enough apart to take a sup. We found a bar which will remain nameless called The Reggae Bar. This unique outdoor bar contained a Thai boxing ring in the middle and between convincing displays of the sport, the referee went about recruiting volunteers to take part. Your reward for fighting was a bucket of their finest, the downside being you could be eating through a straw after the three rounds. Still, the bucket did come with a straw and my drunken decisions staying true to being impeccably bad, I opted to fight.

My opponent was Mike Tyson. Okay, maybe not, but definitely some relation to him. Well, truthfully, he wasn't that either, but he was bigger than me. We were given shorts, gloves and head guards and directed to the toilet to change. I picked blue. As I climbed into the ring it still hadn't occurred to me I had never been in a fight before, let alone even thrown a punch. I warmed up, trying to look like I knew what I was doing as the ref went through the basic rules, and I mean basic as it seemed to me Thai boxing had only one rule – no attacking the crotchal area. The bell sounded and the first punch to my head reminded me of my innocence and that I was also quite drunk. The first round ended as it started with increasing numbers of punches finding my head. I realised I risked total embarrassment in front of the 200 other bargoers who it seemed were taking it more seriously than me at this point, shouting up instructions and advice intended for either 'red' or 'blue'.

My attitude changed as the second round kicked off, my pride on the line – my determination increased. I decided on the game plan of blanket bomb boxing. Basically, I'd punch so much my opponent wouldn't have a chance to punch back so I'd have no need for a defence. In theory, quite a rubbish plan, due to the fact you could only keep it up for so long, as your arms tire quickly. Fortunately, it worked a treat and the perfect punch found his nose and his head found the floor. The bar erupted after longing for any kind of real dramatics to be over-enthusiastic about. The ref stepped in and counted my floored opponent back to his feet. The round then ended and a much needed breather was taken and washed down with water. A third round started and disappeared, both fighters too exhausted to think. The final bell came with the ref's decision to award blue the win. I graciously accepted my free whiskey bucket after probably sweating all the existing alcohol out of my system. I returned to my dressing room/toilet with the adrenaline rush fight night gives you. I have since retired:

Fights 1 Wins 1 Losses 0 Draws 0

But would consider making a comeback if the money was right.

I left the bar through a frenzy of backslapping. It was great to be acknowledged for my unknown and strange fighting skills but my newly sunburnt back wished we had found the back door. I tried to look menacing but this just led to old buddy type hugs which involved a squeeze followed by the backslap. Having escaped my victory, I headed for the water and to a beach bar called Hippies. Drinkers going to Phi Phi will find themselves in this bar at some stage. Continuing until the sun rises, its floor space gradually gets smaller as the tide infringes on the revellers. This is often the sign to strip off and go swimming but I resisted making another bad decision that night, ordered several shots with a vodka bucket chaser and sat/collapsed back to watch the night's entertainers dancing with fire.

*

I wish I had asked her what colour bikini she wore. In the blazing afternoon sun all the girls looked the same on the beach. I walked up and down again hoping she'd spot me, checking girl's faces for slight hints of recognition. Someone eventually recognised me. Smack. Wallop. Backslap. Ouch. "Saw you fight last night". Damn sunburn. But still I didn't see her and it was getting time to leave.

Not far from Phi Phi lies "The Beach", made famous by the movie that's force-fed to you in high dosage on the streets of Bangkok. Mr Garland has probably done more for tourism in this part of the world than the weather. Apparently he's not a fan of the film. Every day full boats aplenty make the trip to the film's real star, where a few hours can be spent sunbathing, swimming or if you've seen the movie, claiming you've just spotted a shark to clear everyone out of the water – hilarious. Even better than all that though and only for a little extra money, you can spend the night on the beach. I only discovered this the night before, after discovering an Irish girl, discover me. Chris

Columbus aside we'd arranged to meet early the next morning to book the trip, the only hiccup coming from the still drunk me. Agreeing separate sober-up sessions were needed, we decided to meet again at three on the beach, which was proving a ridiculous meeting point. Why didn't I suggest the men's toilets? She'd be easily recognisable in there.

*

I waded into the water to get a better perspective of the beach. She was having the same problem and decided also on trying out the panoramic view. We were in line with each other in the water now, a quick glance became a short gaze before we started slowly towards each other.

Is that her I thought or is it another girl who thinks I'm going to try and sell her 'The Beach' on DVD?

Is that him she thought or is he going to try and sell me 'The Beach' on DVD?

We both knew the difficulties we just had but played as if we didn't. Smiles and kisses turned to walking and talking.

"Oh, by the way, do you want to buy 'The Beach' on DVD?" I offered.

"Feck off John".

We made our way back to where we had booked the trip and weren't waiting long for our tour guide to show up. We liked him straight away. Bangkok-born M. Tanned, tattooed, spiky haired and stoned, he arrived on a bicycle and talked like a rapper. He entertained us the short distance to the boat and we were still laughing when we met the ten others we'd be spending the night with. One of them recognised me from a night out in Hanoi. It seemed the world was getting smaller the more I travelled and it wasn't that big to start with. We boarded the boat and tucked into fresh fruit and ice cold beers.

The day trip takes you straight to the bay that encloses the beach but we were headed to the far side of the island where we'd snorkel our way ashore and approach the beach from the back, as Mr Di Caprio did in the film. After a short two hours we were diving into pristine clear warm water, scattering fish in all directions. One by one we reluctantly left our bath, climbed onto the rocks and passed through a cave onto the island's sandy floor. Our boat would meet us on the beach side where we'd set up camp for the night. We excitedly made our way through the wooded area. We'd all seen the movie, most of us had read the book and now we were all here. As we got closer laughter could be heard from the day trippers. The small sandy pathway rounded a final set of palm trees and then opened up onto the beach. We stood there in awe. I imagine the people who were already enjoying the water had the same original reaction, along with the countless previous visitors and those to come. Cliffs on either side continued the beach's curve and standing in the right position it looked like it formed a perfect circle, a bay totally protected from the ocean. From the world outside. We walked into the warm water as our boat arrived into the far side of the bay. The perfectly clear, still water, gave you the illusion it would be possible to walk out to the boat and collect your bag yourself. It wasn't long before the other boats started to return to Phi Phi, taking with them our competition to be lord of the flies. Soon there were 12 people left and I felt so lucky to be one of them.

With all our bags and equipment ashore, a suitable spot was picked to set up camp for the night. To one side of the beach, sheltered by a huge rock face, we erected our tents. Pillows, floor mats and sleeping bags were handed out and our barbecue dinner was started. Music came from an ipod's travel speakers and as the darkness arrived candles were lit illuminating happy faces. Our party was a great mix of nationalities and personalities and we laughed our way through several drinking games after a delicious seafood dinner. As the early hours of the next day approached M suggested we should check out the large crabs that live on the island, not in the warm waters, but on land. We armed ourselves with candles and drunkenly single-filed into the undergrowth. A terrified scream followed by laughter meant we'd found our first. To one side of our trail an orange crab made slow progress in getting away from us. His two huge pincers made you think twice before picking him up, a wrong movement and he'd surely have your finger off. After careful study, we let him on his way and decided if he wasn't going to make use of the beautiful waters, we certainly were. We raced back through our camp site and submerged ourselves into the warmest night sea I've ever been in. Beers were handed out and we drank and floated as best we could until sleep made us leave this perfect day behind.

Not long after my eyes shut in the tent, they were open again. My Irish friend had already been up at first light which I figured was about five minutes ago.

"There's no one on the beach," she whispered, "it's all yours".

I crawled from my sleeping bag and out of the tent. The light, although a dull grey, still hurt my eyes. The beach was deserted and as I left the camp site the only sound was that of the small waves lapping onto the white sand. I walked to the far end, where it started to curve like a slow turning bend, and I took a seat on the now cool sand. Paradise found, I thought, as I looked back on where I had come from – the tents silent with sleep or maybe a little further, Dublin.

The boat trip back to Phi Phi swayed some of us to sleep and others with the promise of keeping in touch. Agreement was made on what a perfect night we had had. People, a place and a certain time seemed to line up in perfect symmetry that night.

Phi Phi was still graced in the sunny magnificence we'd left it in and it seemed no matter how many times you left, it would always be this welcoming. Over the previous few days I had passed a sign on my way to my guest house for 'The Lookout'. A steep set of cement steps showed you the way and what you should expect. It wasn't too long before my muscles were burning from the sudden exertion and the energy-sapping heat. But

I have always loved the views you have to work at to see. I feel slightly like a cheat if all I do is press an elevator button and wait a patient minute to gain my view. Trees covered any sight of the surrounding island there might have been, it was the view from the top or nothing at all. I was really enjoying myself as I passed a red-faced couple with a look of betrayal that dripped sweat. A sign for ice cream faced me as I turned the last corner. I'd say plenty of it was sold up here but I'd hate to be the delivery man. Not disappointed and worth the effort, the view was stunning. Both beaches were visible with the town intersecting between the two. Just how much destruction a wave can do, hit home. Apart from ice cream, the tourist shop also sold DVDs. I picked up one, 'Phi Phi – The Tsunami'. On the back of every tragedy there will always be someone lining their pockets.

*

I was in the middle of an argument with time. It wouldn't stop and I wouldn't go. My flight from Singapore to Australia was fast approaching and being stubborn to the last I had missed any possible flights I could have availed of from Krabi to Singapore. I checked the clock one more time. Still ticking. I admitted defeat and booked a bus. I didn't want to leave, had already stayed longer than I should have and with great company. But I knew she felt the same. We had shared some of the best times since I boarded my first flight. I may have had a camera full of photos now, but it's never the same. I wanted to continue to see her, touch her, be in her. I was close to tears when I knew it was time for the last kiss goodbye. I slowly looked down, got on my knees and kissed the pier.

"Phi Phi, I'll miss you".

My friend laughed, "you really are strange John, take care babe".

We kissed and I was gone.

Singapore (and the road to)

As the boat arrived back to the mainland I was feeling strangely upbeat about the 24-hour bus journey ahead of me. Buses in Thailand are renowned for their comfort compared to the rest of Asia and from what I'd already experienced, even compared to back home. On seeing now what would become my day, my night and my next day, I joined the small group of four staring blankly at it. We looked at each other, knowing we shared the same fate and probably the same thought.

'If we load our bags on, will there be enough room for us?'

I took a walk around it, making sure it wasn't an optical illusion. No, I was now as sure as the driver was – we'd be heading to Singapore in a Hi Ace Van. On the up side, they'd seen fit to install seats, possibly thinking it would be too much to ask anyone to sit on a metal floor for 24 hours and charge them for the privilege. We squeezed our bags, then ourselves inside and held in our breaths to avail the slamming of the door shut. Parking on a downward slope had been the driver's clever way of disguising the van's need for a push start, but soon, and to the sweet smell of gasoline, we were headed south.

Two of the group were asleep in no time, barely a mile between bus and boat. That left me and a couple from England and since the van's space constraints were causing me to involuntarily nibble on her neck, I thought it would be less awkward on all to make conversation. It turned out we had travelled Asia, visiting the same places, but two weeks apart. Conscious a sudden jolt of the van could end up with a love bite on her neck from a stranger, she wisely brushed her hair over to my side. We talked about tubing, the bars and the swings. The same swing I had asked about had snapped when they were there, less than 14 days after me. No wonder the guy laughed at me. The unlucky was lucky enough to just suffer bad bruising. I dozed off with a lock of brown hair tickling my nose.

The van's sliding door woke me with a sneeze. Luckily the driver had stopped first before walking around the other side and opening the door. With the mention of transferring to another bus I got excited. We were asked to hand over our tickets and then we clambered out to inspect our new luxury vehicle. No, still a Hi Ace. The drivers had a chat, our tickets were passed to the new driver and we were told that this particular fine machine would now take us to Singapore. We re-squeezed bags and bodies and were off again.

Hardly a bite taken from our 24 hours and we were again stopping. The same routine took place with our tickets being handed over to a new driver of a same ole Hi Ace. We soon worked out our tickets were being bought and sold like shares on the stock exchange and whoever ended up with them in Singapore cashed them in. This seemed pretty apt since we were heading to Nick Leeson's adopted home where he single-handedly brought down the UK's oldest investment bank, Baring's. We just hoped our tickets were worth enough now to get us all the way there.

Two more bus exchanges later and we finally made it to the Malaysian border. It was time to fill out more forms and declare we had nothing to declare so we could swiftly move along. Malaysians are strict on two issues concerning us entering their country – cigarettes and chewing gum. They don't like you bringing in either. Of course if you happen to have a half pack of Wrigley's Extra you sensibly say nothing and they're none the wiser, not that you'd get arrested for being minty fresh. Unfortunately things didn't quite go to plan and we were left waiting for an hour on one of the girls who decided she did have something to declare. After more then 20 hours already in various so-called buses, the mood wasn't the best among us. She finally made her way onto the bus.

"What happened?" I asked.

"I thought it was best that I declared my cigarettes," she said.

"How many?"

"Five," she coughed hinting embarrassment.

"Five packs, yeah?"

"Ah, no, just five cigarettes".

She knew when she said it how stupid it was and right now, how stupid she was. There was no need for me to tell her, as much as I wanted to. Our already cramped space seemed to get smaller, a nervous cough was all that broke the tired silence.

28 hours and 5 buses later we rolled into Singapore. Hardly slept and wearing the same clothes as yesterday or maybe the day before, I had already picked a hostel so found a taxi to take me there. My accommodation was in the Indian Quarter, one of the cheapest places to stay here, so it was alive with other back-packers. After a power nap and a weak shower I took advantage of the reduced-priced drinks at the bar for anyone staying there. The English couple joined me for a few drinks, having not taken my neck nibbling to heart, and we made our way to Clarke Quay, the apparent heart of Singaporean night life.

Much like Hong Kong, this place wasn't really suited to a backpacker budget, but it seemed to lack the charm that convinced you you didn't mind spending more than you had. The city seemed sterile and clinical. Almost like blocks of Lego had been placed together and when more Lego was bought, the city expanded. The place was spotless, not a dried chewing gum blob on the path to be seen. But instead of giving you the appearance of being very clean, there was more a sense of it not being lived in. Like the perfectly put together showhouse, which is just four walls until someone moves in, makes their own mess and declares it a home. I couldn't find anything homely about Singapore.

We decided on a few drinks in the suitably named bar, The Clinic. Running with the hospital theme, the seats were golden-coloured wheelchairs, the tables were separated by curtains and the famous 'Sex on the beach' cocktail, was now 'Sex on a drip' – literally. I couldn't justify the $50 it would cost to suck alcohol from a tube so had to make do with a normal beer. I was getting used to my wheelchair and found it hard to keep still. I wanted to see how fast I could go. It didn't escape the attention of the waiter and not wanting to lose a seat, he positioned himself beside me. This didn't stop me from trying though, I feigned left and took off to my right, my arms pumping the wheels. Quick as a drip though I was caught and wheeled back to the clinic. Usually I didn't want to leave bars and now I didn't want to stay.

I was leaving for Australia the next day and was glad because I had no inkling to hang around. I had heard Singapore airport was pretty impressive so I think it says something about my overall impression of the city, when I say I was looking forward to checking it out. With the promise of a whole new continent to contend with, I slept contently.

Chapter 7

THE DRUGS DON'T WORK

Cairns

A good few years ago, while in London for a week, I met an Australian girl. She was living there for the year and prior to returning home she visited Dublin. Before she left she asked me to go to Australia with her, offering to pay for the flight, with a free place to stay when I got there. I had to turn it down. I had just recorded a CD which was being released the following month, I couldn't leave. For my next birthday she sent me 'A rough guide to Melbourne' and a card asking when was I going to visit? A lot happened in the years that followed, I never made it to Australia, the band broke up, and myself and the girl from Melbourne lost touch. This is what I was thinking as the plane touched Australian tarmac. Maybe I should let her know I'd eventually made it.

Customs were friendly but firm. Read the sign and know what you can't bring into the country, right down to the mud on your boots. My turn came and I handed over my passport.

"G'day," made me smile, "you've been to a lot of countries," he remarked, "a lot of drugs in those countries."

"Eh, I'd say there is, yeah," I responded.

"Did you bring any with you?" he asked.

I had to weigh up my answer here. With most Australian people I had previously met, this kind of sense of humour would be right up their street, but this was an airport, this was customs, surely no joking about.

"No, course not," I replied.

"Pity," he winked, "but I will have to cut open your balls."

"Sorry?" I gulped.

"Your juggling balls, where'd you get them?"

"Ah, Bangkok," I breathed again.

He cut along the seam of one and its seedy inside spilled out.

"You can't bring seeds into our country mate."

There went my circus audition.

A short bus ride from the airport dropped me into the centre of Cairns. The wide streets were alive with sunshine as I checked into my hostel. The apparent five star Gilligans was meant to be upmarket accommodation for backpackers, boasting a swimming pool, bar and, to my annoyance, key cards for the rooms. My first card sent me to the third floor and refused to open the door. A return to reception gave me a change of room, this one on the second floor, the key card worked but each of the six beds were already in use. Once again down to reception and a third room on the fourth floor. Finally getting a bed, the fact that half the lights didn't work could wait.

After a couple of hours with my eyes shut I left the hostel to check out the town. In the last few months I had grown fond of the Asian streets and buildings and now I had that all too familiar feeling I was back in Dublin. The price of a mug of coffee didn't help and for the first time since I left I was very conscious of money, and I hate money. It's a necessary evil though, that often brings out the worst in people and if I wasn't careful it would send me home early and bring out the worst in me. Bearing this in mind, I decided it would be cheaper to drink more in the hostel before venturing out to the bars, so a bottle of vodka was in order. I had barely made the counter when the 20-something male working there proclaimed, "Mate, are you wearing mascara?"

Now, I'm aware I have very dark eyelashes and have been since I was 15, but I'm more used to stares or glances back home rather than a straight up question – that usually comes when the curious is drunk enough. I laughed and explained I wasn't but this just roused the curiosity of everyone else in the shop. After posing for inspection I bought the vodka and left. I liked that about the Australians though, they definitely weren't shy.

That night I had a few vodka cokes in the hostel, followed by a few more. In half an hour, half the bottle was gone and I felt as I did when I started. Drinking buckets in Asia had sent my tolerance for alcohol through the roof, which would unfortunately have a direct impact on my wallet. This wasn't good, so I addressed the situation over the rest of the bottle and came up with a cunning plan – it was time to switch to wine. I returned to my room and it was no surprise when my key card didn't work. I thought for a second, was I on the right floor or not, then once again made my way to the unhelpful reception.

The reason I came to Cairns and the reason I did a diving course in Vietnam was so I could dive the Great Barrier Reef. I had been advised to go to the outer reef because it would be less packed. I presumed this meant less people than less fish so after booking a day trip I was now here. We were told we'd be stopping at three dive sites where we could scuba and snorkel, and in between those, there was plenty of food and sun. We were divided into groups and given 'buddies', I being slightly more suspicious of that concept now. But soon we were among the sea life, swimming round boulders with multi-coloured fish. After returning to the boat I joined others, snorkelling. The captain asked everyone to swim to one side of the boat and when we were in position he threw in food. Within seconds baby sharks appeared. Several people made for the boat in fright. Although the rest of us knew they wouldn't touch us, it was just unnerving to see a nose coming towards you and turning in avoidance at the last moment.

My plan was to make it to Sydney for Christmas. Many of my newly made friends would be there too. The cheapest way to travel was by bus, so I purchased a Greyhound ticket. The timetable told me the towns it stopped in and when. All I had to do was give them 24 hours' notice and a seat was mine. With that, I was leaving Cairns and starting my journey down Australia's east coast.

Magnetic Island

Something was drawing me to Magnetic Island. I'm unaware of any foreign metal objects lodged inside me, so I put it down to curiosity. I got off the bus in Townsville, which is seen as the unofficial capital of North Queensland, where I'd spend the night and in the morning catch the boat. Walking the streets I noticed something I hadn't seen in the last few months – bouncers. Every bar I passed had one sporting the typical black attire and unfriendly sulky appearance. I made to walk past one and was stopped.

"No thongs in here, mate," he growled.

I think it would be best if I clarified that I'm not a cross dresser that forgot to get fully dressed. Thongs in Australia are what we call flip flops. I had lived in mine the last few months, my feet had never known such freedom. I had forgotten how bad socks could smell. Sockygen. What is it about bouncers and footwear the world over? At home I could be stopped for wearing runners but shoes are okay, here, no flip flops but runners are okay. I made a mental note to go to Amsterdam and buy clogs to confuse the fuckers. Meanwhile a girl had appeared and was asking the bouncers for directions, presumably for the nearest shoe shop. A pair of breasts were enough to distract him and obviously not being able to process more than one interaction at a time, I walked past him and into the crowded bar.

Australian Rules football jerseys on the wall were all that differed to a bar back home. Then again, I thought, it could easily be an Australian bar in Dublin. The sway from the packed crowd seemed to bring me towards the bar, where I'd buy a cocktail, and away again, where I'd drink it. I let this nauseous circle repeat itself a few times before I'd had enough of listening to the arrogance of the surrounding Australian blokes, each one trying to be louder than the next as if it was some sort of primal mating call. I had grown cheekier with each drink so as I was leaving I made a point of addressing the bouncer.

"Thanks for that," I chirped.

"Eh, you can't come in here," he cleverly retorted.

"That's why I'm leaving," I smiled.

Utter confusion crossed his face until he spotted a bouncing pair cross the road.

The next morning I joined a packed boat for the short journey across to Magnetic Island and once we landed we each sought out our accommodation. The island, only 52km squared, isn't very big. I decided to rent a car so I could leisurely drive around it. With its many beaches there are plenty of places to swim so I also rented a mask, snorkel, flippers and a very attractive stinger suit since I was told it was jelly fish season. Stopping at my first beach and suiting up I couldn't help think I looked like Steve Zizzu from the Life Aquatic, so a quick dash was made to the cover of the ocean. After a day spent exploring the sea in several different places, I was ravenous so returned to my hostel for dinner.

The next day I noticed a sign by reception. "Free night's stay plus food and drink for anyone who volunteers to work in the kitchen." This immediately appealed to my now budget-conscious self, and I reckoned I had plenty of experience having always washed my own plates and mugs after use, sometimes even dried them too. I eagerly signed up and with a smile was told to report to the kitchen at six. That left me the afternoon and I had a sudden urge to hit something.

Not far from the hostel was a golf course. I'd be a fair weather golfer and today the weather couldn't have been fairer with pure blue skies and tan temperatures. I rented a set of clubs and declined the offer of a caddy car. I was a man after all. Strong and fit enough to carry my own bag, well, at least to the small motorised vehicle I had also just rented. I sat in, put my foot down and I was on my way. Then I realised I hadn't teed off yet, that this was a golf course and not a go-kart track, so I selected a club and missed the ball – twice. Proceedings started slow, got slower, stopped for awhile when I had to go looking for my ball and then I finally made it to the second tee. I checked my scorecard and was quite pleased with myself. For the nine hole golf course I was currently looking good at 25 under par and I suspected in line for a course record. Having said that, I had only played one hole where I'd gotten a ten. The next two holes saw to it that my dream round was crushed and I eventually finished out the round well out of contention for qualifying for next year's PGA tour. Still, my tan had come on nicely.

I drove back to the hostel to report for work. *Bless me, my wallet, for I have been a slacker, it's been five months since I've done a tap.* As soon as I walked into the kitchen I didn't like the mood. It felt like I'd just walked into a trap and was about to be taken advantage of, which I was of course. I completed a four-man line up, two of which were women. Pleasantries aside (there were none) I was thrown an apron and told to get scrubbing the dishes. The boss was a girl, no more than my own age, who seemed to take delight in shouting, bullying and basically being a bitch. I felt sorry for the two full-time staff who seemed too afraid to even make eye contact with me. I got to work thinking as soon as I got through the waiting pile of dishes I could get out of there, but as soon as I made any headway into them, more arrived. My hands were pure black now as if I'd been working on a car's engine rather than used pots and pans. Every so often on-the-spot inspections took place and the boss enjoyed reintroducing washed pots for a second bath. Finally after four hours I was allowed to leave, my dinner in hand. To think at one point, a much younger me had aspirations of becoming a chef. I was going to take advantage of my free bed tonight. A phone call was made and a seat on a bus awaited me the next day.

Whit Sundays

Two things had started to become obvious to me. One, unlike Asia where your age and general status in life doesn't matter a peg to anyone, here it seemed I was answering those questions to everyone I met and since they brought up the age issue, I'd have to say they all seemed ten years younger than me. When I finished school, a two-week holiday in the Spanish sun seemed to be the norm, now school leavers are taking over the Australian east coast and thinking it strange to be in the presence of a 30-year-old, all the while trying to decide which one of Daddy's credit cards they would use today – the blue one or the black one?

Secondly, I realised there was no escaping this. It was like we were all on a giant escalator carrying us down the east coast, hopping off and jumping back on in the same places. The bus journey to Airlie Beach was filled with familiar faces, the town bringing more when I got there. I joined the queue in the hostel to confirm my reservation – yes, I really did exist, and I still needed a bed. I reluctantly paid out $25 for one half of a bunk bed in a room with 11 other people. When I got to my bed there were no sheets or pillow present so I rejoined the reception scrum.

"I just checked my bed, there's no sheets or pillow," I innocently said.

"It's $5 to rent them and a $5 deposit."

"Sorry, you serious?"

Her stony silence confirmed that she was.

"Any bed you rent anywhere, comes with sheets and a pillow," I tried, getting angry.

"Not here," she said.

"And a deposit too, do you think I'm going to rob your pillow?"

This attitude was starting to get to me. Backpackers are being seriously ripped off and by extremely unfriendly staff. Not one mention of this in the guide books. Who is writing the reports? The staff? A backpackers' union of the world is needed. I thought about Asia as my head touched the pillow, I thought about stealing.

I booked my place on the Atlantic Clipper, a boat with a party reputation. Each of us were given canvas bags so we could take on board the essentials needed. We were under strict instructions not to bring any bag with a zip because apparently this is the bed bug's favourite form of transport, when they weren't taking it easy in bed, I assume. Also, glass bottles were prohibited for obvious reasons – they didn't burn as well as plastic bottles when we started an illegal bonfire on one of the environmentally protected islands. I joined the queue to board the boat, having stopped off at the inappropriately named Bottle Shop, to buy cans, of course. Behind me a girl was in conversation, I recognised the accent.

"Whereabouts are you from?" I asked.

"Meath," she smiled.

"Ashbourne by any chance?" I replied.

"Yeah that's right!"

I mentioned my night spent on The Beach accompanied by a girl from Ashbourne.

"Oh my God, you're John," she exploded.

They turned out to be best friends and she had just left Sydney where they had celebrated her birthday together. As the walls of the world drew closer together, I boarded a confined space.

With everyone settled and relaxed, a beer in hand the cause of both, the captain introduced the crew and explained our plotted course on a giant map he had spread out on the deck. Rations were then distributed and I drank my fill of vodka orange juices hoping I could get enough vitamin C into me so I wouldn't develop scurvy over the course of the three days at sea.

I woke early the next morning with scurvy. My panic subsided though when it turned out to be just a hangover and even that soon subsided after a good dose of ocean air. The night had seen us gain ground on our specifically plotted course, well, either that or they had forgotten to anchor the boat while we slept, but I believed we were in the hands of professionals. Whit Sunday Island was now to be seen not far from the boat. The order came from the captain which sent the crew into a frenzy. Beers and snorkelling gear were handed out while we boarded dinghys to take us ashore. I drank my beer through my snor-

kel and fell overboard. Luckily the dinghy had already reached
the beach so the worst that happened to me was getting a new
kind of dandruff. Sandruff. There was no need for the attractive stinger suits this time and I was soon enjoying the aquarium
life. Food was thrown from the dinghy and you'd be surrounded
by dozens of colourful hungry fish in seconds. Shortly it was
time to see the real attraction of the island. A path led us into
the undergrowth and up a hilly incline. On the far side a pure
white sandy beach awaited us. I had seen it on a postcard before
I left and to see it now in front of us made us reach for a beer
before we reached the water. The afternoon was spent splashing
about, being dried off by the sun and inventing our own sport
that combined Australian Rules, American football, Snakes and
Ladders and a Frisbee. Exhausted, we made it back to the boat
as darkness spread along the sky. To our delight, dolphins swam
beside the boat as we made our way back to Airlie Beach. It was
time to jump back onto the conveyor belt and hop off again at
the next designated stop.

Fraser Island

The backpacker trail led me to Hervey Bay where a short boat
trip would land me on Fraser Island the following day. It's the
largest sand island in the world, stretching 123km long, and
was first discovered by Captain Cook in 1770 while opening a
can of beans for breakfast. I had already paid in full and this
included two nights in a hostel either side of the Fraser stay.
I booked in and was impressed with the modern interior. As
well as clean bright rooms, a large kitchen area was topped by
a comfy TV room with plenty of DVDs to choose from. I had
just settled in for the night when I received a text from home. A
home-grown celeb had died from a cocaine overdose. Outside
the backpacker's bubble, life was still continuing and coming to
an end.

Early the next morning I joined the rest of the Fraser Island party. We met in reception for a talk about the coming days. We were being given a Jeep that came with serious rules about driving safely on sand. We combined our money and filled it with food and drink supplies, then joined other Jeeps in the queue for the ferry. Once we touched down on sand the different parties fled off in various directions until it became obvious there was but one sand highway and this was soon jammed. Consulting our map we decided our first stop would be lunch by one of the 40 freshwater lakes found on Fraser and it was such a good idea everyone else had it too. After a swim in the warm salt free water we retired to a picnic bench for lunch. We had been warned about the wild dingos that roamed the island freely and no sooner had we made some sandwiches, than they were eyeing us up from a distance.

Our accommodation on the island was an Aborigine camp site. It was apparently the only place you could legally light a camp fire there, so we were looking forward to toasting marshmallows after dinner. A circular room housed enough camp beds for us all so we had no need for the tents. An outdoor kitchen had everything we'd need to cook a feed but in every available space it seemed, spiders had made their mark with giant webs, and as the night fell they arrived home. Doing our best to ignore the uninvited guests we tucked into our freshly cooked hamburgers and produced dice and cards to play drinking games. After, as we sat around our open fire realising someone forgot to pack the marshmallows, the two Aborigines who looked after the camp site arrived. They had dressed up, or down even, with white chalky paint covering their dark skin. Introductions were made and the older, Travis, asked where I was from. On hearing I was Irish his face lit up.

"I'm Irish too, mate," he glowed.

"Really, what's your surname?"

"O'Farrell," he said proudly, "grandfather was from Longford."

He proved he had as much of a grasp of the Irish language as I have, which isn't extensive but pretty impressive coming from an Aborigine living on Fraser Island. He then decided it was time to dance and being Irish we should stick together. Much to the amusement of the rest, I stumbled through the movements of four different songs. Before each, the meaning behind them was explained. When we returned to the fire, Travis asked us to observe two Aborigine rules while sitting there. He didn't want us to spit into the fire or whistle when near it. According to Aboriginal folklore, both can upset the spirits. We did our own version of upsetting spirits and finished a couple of bottles of vodka before climbing into our camp beds in torch light, after a quick check for spiders.

The early morning light outlined an unwanted guest, his numerous hairy legs creeping over one of the cross beams above our heads. Suddenly everyone was wide awake, ready for breakfast and dressed in record time. We'd worry about him later. After eating, we made our way down to the beach where the shipwrecked boat Eliza Fraser sits since 1836, the reason for the Island's name. Further on, the sand got too deep to drive over. Several Jeeps had already been stranded and abandoned by their occupiers. We continued on foot to the Champagne Baths, a large rock pool, heated to bath temperature by the sun and every few minutes covered in spray by waves crashing in from the sea. Our afternoon was spent hurling wet balls of sand at each other and talking about our lives back home.

It wasn't long before we were packing up our Jeep and saying our goodbyes. Travis explained that for Aborigines there are no goodbyes only farewells because they believe they'll always meet again.

"How about slán?" I asked.

He smiled, "slán a cháirde."

We made it back to the ferry to join the queue to park. With everyone on board we headed back to Hervey Bay, looking forward to a hot shower.

Nimbin

I boarded the greyhound bus and spotted a familiar face I was delighted to see – the driver. Light blue shirt, navy shorts and white socks to his knees he looked the pommie part but it was his sense of humour and familiar sounding voice that appealed to me. He liked to talk about the town we were heading to over the bus's intercom, listing places of interest he knew full well no backpacker would ever see, in his deadpan Clive James drawl. His dry wit had me doubled up as he listed the merits of a glass factory over a backpacker bar.

My stop was the very popular Byron Bay, but that's not where I intended to stay. I hoped to catch a bus inland to a town called Nimbin I'd read about. In the '70s Nimbin hosted its own Woodstock festival. It went so well that people didn't leave when it was over. A commune started and over the years it has grown into a single-streeted town with enough people to merit a small police station. The interesting thing is that the town still seems to be stuck in its festival decade. Like I spotted on Khao San road, the young hippies have grown older but their way of life has remained the same. Nowadays their principal earner is drugs. You can't walk from over there to somewhere over here without being offered a bag of grass or some home made cookies and not like your mother used to make them either. Furthermore, if the interest takes you, there's a museum that gives you the history of hash and of course a gift shop on the way out just in case you want a souvenir joint. As I mentioned, there are police and they're not altogether stupid. They know what Nimbin is all about. But just to keep some sort of balance between their two faux jobs they go through a daily ritual which involves the police taking a drive down the main street. As soon as they're spotted a shout can be heard that echoes along the footpath. 'Taxi'. As it's passed on, dealers disappear but it's soon business as usual when the police return to their station. Nimbin doesn't have any taxis.

I said farewell to Clive James as he insisted I checked out a paper bag factory and made my way to a bus stop where I found panic. It turned out there was only one bus a day to Nimbin and it had already been missed. To make things worse there was no accommodation to be had anywhere. Desperate phone calls were made throughout the large group of backpackers but to no avail and as the evening closed in there was talk of sleeping on the beach. I got talking to two English guys who had the same intentions of making Nimbin. We agreed paying for a taxi was slightly more appealing than sleeping rough, so we went about finding one.

Apart from the panicked crowd at the bus stop there was also a small group of worse for wear Aborigines who seemed to have already consumed a vast amount of their home-made alcoholic brew. This made for an uneasy feeling as the rest discussed what to do for the night. I managed to get a taxi a short way down the road, jumped in and drove back to the English lads at the bus stop. As they were loading the bags in the back, the loudest Aborigine swung a stick he was carrying and struck one of them square in the jaw. The attack was totally unprovoked and he sat into the back seat in shock. When we all realised what had happened the taxi driver waved it off as a common occurrence. He said it was pointless going to the police as the Aborigines were a law unto themselves, getting away with far worse than that all the time.

The taxi took us inland where the small road was covered by greenery on both sides. It twisted and turned for an hour and a half until the once hippy commune came into view. We chose a hostel that was slightly outside the town, which meant we were in the middle of nowhere. We passed a tepee on the drive up and arrived in, hungry, hot and one of us sore-jawed. As expected, the atmosphere was very relaxed. We waited in the empty reception area for several minutes but no one showed up, so we took a walk round back. There, a long wooden table was occupied on either side. We were noticed and waved over invitingly.

"We'd like to book in."

"No worries, I'll show you your room," the absent receptionist said as he disappeared inside.

We followed him in and as we reached our dorm he spun
around.

"Is this enough?" he smiled.

In his hand swung a bag of grass. Welcome to Nimbin.

We soon adapted to the daily routine that was so adamantly
adhered to by the seasoned guests. Bed was left by midday and a
caffeine fix came in the form of an over-sized mug. As everyone
started to surface and gather in the garden, the day's first joints
were rolled. Neglecting to eat, it wasn't long before the effect
was felt and spread by laughter. A game of monopoly would be
started with best intentions but would soon break down and
fail to make sense as the influence bar got higher and we slipped
under it. Four hours of properties being bought, exchanged and
taken over by the bank, of house and hotel empires being built
from scratch, of jail time done and lotteries won, someone then
asked why was there a dog on the board? We exploded into
convulsions of ludicrous laughter, falling from our chairs, trying to catch our breath and get our heads around the monopoly
maker's decision of character choice.

Recovered enough to have dropped the intensity of laughter
to a giggle, we realised we were starving. The hostel's van was
commandeered and we made the short trip into the town. It was
only late afternoon so there was plenty of time for two dinners.
With spaghetti bolognese for a starter and steak for the main
decided on, we returned to make a mess in the kitchen. Each
course was followed with a joint and full up on food a round of
coffees were made to accompany a movie or those brave enough
to attempt a game of chess. The night continued and as the cal-
endar declared a new day the darkness was dotted with glowing
ash. I inhaled and briefly glowed the brightest.

In the last few months I found it increasingly difficult to keep track of which day it was and now it was a complete mystery. When I thought about it, I wasn't exactly sure how long I'd been here. The day had an identical twin, or triplet or quad. I had used Nimbin as a kind of rehab. Before Christmas a few days off drink would be a good idea, which I had easily managed to do by replacing one drug with another. I wasn't sure this was the best road to go down so the argument to go back on the drink was a good one. I sat contemplating all this, looking out along a valley of Australian wilderness, feeling the sun heat my bones. Beside me sat a Russian, at least we all thought he was. His English was terrible and since I had arrived he had been too stoned to talk anyway. He sat with us through the days and joined in as much as he could. Laughed when we laughed. Smoked when we smoked and also when we didn't smoke. Now the owner was among us, she needed to know who was going to be around for Christmas. A show of hands went around the table, the Russian didn't move. She was used to this so she moved closer and explained her question directly to him. We waited, watching his face. Suddenly his red sunken eyes displayed acknowledgement.

"It is Christmas?" His genuine surprise was evident through his thick accent. This brought a laugh amongst the others. He had probably left home with the best intentions of travelling Australia and now here he was, weeks, maybe even months later, in the world of mind-numbing Nimbin. This wasn't for me. As he nodded his agreement to continue his vocation, I decided it was time to leave.

Chapter 8

A SHIP CALLED DIGNITY

Sydney

It was the run up to Christmas now. Back home the panic for last minute presents was forming queues the retailers loved and the customers hated. I was sitting on an air conditioned bus slowly making its way through Sydney's suburbs thinking how unChristmasy it felt. When I first landed in Cairns the question on where I was going to stay over Christmas came up. I hadn't thought about it. My last minute long finger attitude back home was suited well to life on the road up until now. When I discovered some had booked accommodation as early as the summer months before, I thought it best to at least have a look. Shockingly, hostels were charging a $100 a night with a stipulation of staying a minimum of ten nights. I couldn't do that. Apart from the money, what if I didn't like the place? So after some high speed searching I found a single room with a shared bathroom in the well known King's Cross area for five nights at $300. The area is famous for its bars and strip clubs, but it was coffee shops that lined the street either side of my guest house and, with the underground just around the corner, it was perfect.

That night I decided to check out the bars, but the strip clubs would have to wait as I was meeting a Cork man, all the way from Clonakilty, I'd met on my day diving the Barrier Reef. He had been working in Sydney, had taken some time out to travel the east coast and now was back for the festive season. After pub crawling one part of town we decided to return to King's Cross and in the taxi en route a drunken topic of how we could tell Irish women from Australian women arose. The taxi driver was quite amused by this banter but didn't believe us. With that, we stopped at a set of traffic lights and sure enough two girls we suspected as being Irish were there waiting to cross. My friend rolled down the window to prove a point.

"Where you from?" he shouted over.

"Ireland," came the reply.

"I'm from Ireland, whereabouts?"

"Cork."

"I'm from Cork, whereabouts?"

"Clonakilty."

"I'm from Clonakilty!"

"Where are you's going?" they excitedly asked while approaching the car.

The baffled taxi man hadn't noticed the lights turn green.

"Quick, go, go," he was shouted at.

"Yeah buoy, that was a close one," my friend managed before we fell into hysterics. Of all the street corners, in all the world.

As we closed the door of the taxi, a bouncer stood in our way from opening the door of the club. I checked my footwear and was happy I remembered to put some on, even happier when I noticed they were shoes.

"Not tonight lads," he said before I could even wipe the satisfied smile from my face.

"It can't be footwear, what is it?"

"Too many guys inside already."

"What? So if we were women you'd let us in?"

"Course," he replied, "let you in even if you have women with you mate."

Now it was our turn to be baffled. It was time for some life altering surgery or find a date in a city I had just arrived in. I quite fancied the challenge of the latter but we decided instead to go somewhere we'd be very welcome.

"Which way did you say that strip club was?"

*

'And the bells were ringing out for Christmas Day'. We sang like it was the last song we'd get to sing and loud enough to drown out any bells. The Christmas feeling had arrived with the early hours of Christmas Day and a tray of shots. The Irish bar was crammed with people of both varieties – those who were Irish and those who wanted to be. But Irish or not it didn't matter. It was Christmas Day and most were far from home. Our friends and drinking buddies were now all promoted to family on this day. My adopted family came in the form of Lee, an English guy living in Sydney and whom I met while travelling around Asia. We kept in touch and he generously invited me along to his friend's apartment for Christmas dinner. After, I'd hoped anyway, a few hours' sleep, I'd catch the morning ferry to Manly. As I left the bar the heat hit me and seemed to melt away any Christmasy feeling.

Another beautiful morning embraced me as I caught the ferry to Manly, just across the bay. I noticed champagne being toasted in plastic cups and matching Santa hats and thought about home. Lee was waiting for me as I left the boat. It was great to see him again and we caught up as we made our way to his friend's place. I joined 14 others on the apartment's rooftop garden. I liked them straight away. Here was a group of people who had left where they were from to start a new life in Sydney. In the corner a pig was slowly turning and cooking on a spit, the centre piece of today's feast. We enjoyed the afternoon like a band of Robin Hood's merry men, eating and drinking our fill and toasting to good times. I had also arranged to meet friends from home on the popular Coogee beach, so as night fell I bid my Aborigine farewells and caught the ferry.

By the time I'd made it there, the beach was in chaos. It seemed like every Irish person in the city had convened here early this morning and had skipped the Christmas dinner. Some were getting sick where they sat, while others slept where they drank. I could feel tension in the air, this wasn't a place full of the festive spirit. Sure enough, a fight kicked off. As the brawl moved about, it came in contact with the different circular groups dotted randomly around, and each time it did, it grew in size. We soon figured out it was a bunch of Donegal lads against the rest. This was the drink-fuelled bravado that I don't do, and besides, it was Christmas.

Just like back home, Stephen's Day here is all about the races and with free admission for anyone with an Irish passport, we were sold. Everyone was in high spirits as the champagne mixed with the sun and bets were made. We scanned the race card like seasoned gamblers trying to pick a winner, but in my case, to no avail. I've just never been much good at gambling. A second bottle of champagne seemed to talk sense into me and I curtailed my abuse of money but realised a talking champagne bottle wasn't the best sign. When there were no more horses to bet on we made it back into the city to bet on our livers surviving the night.

New Year's Eve crept up on me as quickly as a dental appointment. I lay back and opened wide. Alcohol was poured straight from the bottle until I spluttered and turned away, leaving a sticky green line from mouth to ear. I had rejoined Lee and his band of merry friends for the night's celebrations. A venue was chosen, a jazz club not too far from Sydney harbour, and tickets were purchased. The night's entertainment was a funk band called 'Brown Sugar' and they didn't disappoint. In fact, the songs were so good you had to force yourself to leave the dance floor to have a drink. As the night went on I felt I was getting fitter instead of drunker. Soon a new year was only minutes away. The band took a break and cocktails were bought in proportion to how many free hands you had. I bought four. Not that I had sprouted a couple more hands overnight, just that over the years you pick up various bar skills. In a drunken haze it's incredible how diligently the human brain can work. In only the few minutes it can take to get an order of drinks communicated to the appropriate person, the following delicate decisions are made at lightning speed:

What do I want?
How many of it do I want?
How many can I realistically carry?
Will that girl kiss me if I buy her one too?
If not, how many would I have to buy her to eventually get that kiss?
Where are the toilets again?
I wonder if the bar girl is single?
Do I smell a kebab?

All questions answered to satisfaction in my head, I followed the crowd to the street outside and as if making a sit down protest against marrow fat peas we took up every inch of the road facing Sydney bridge. The count down was counted down rather than up, even though we were on the other side of the world and as it concluded the sights and sounds of what could have been the end of the world scribbled and echoed through the sky. Sydney is the first major city to ring in the new year, which it does with furious gusto each year, seemingly aware the world's eyes are upon them in jealous awe. Our faces lit up and changed colour corresponding with the fireworks. Red faces turned to green as I looked around but the expressions of delight remained intact. As the entertainment came to a close 'Brown Sugar' once again took to the stage and those still able to walk, ran back inside. We danced in circles, holding each other up, singing words written in the '70s and belted to life in 2008. Apart from a new year celebration I knew what this was – a goodbye to Sydney, a goodbye to my new friend Lee. He knew it too. We raised our glasses and hoped the remaining days of this innocent year would live up to its beginning.

"Mate, you're a legend."

I had sent the email and received a reply so I booked a flight to a place I'd previously heard The Edge sing about, where one of their wildlife had featured on a chocolate bar I used to eat as a kid. And most importantly, where Mel and Malcolm lived – my Vietnamese Tasmanian friends.

Tasmania

As I collected my bag from the carousel I was greeted by a dog. This was a dog that had learnt there was more to sniff in this world then other dogs' butts. There were whole airport arrival halls filled with people with bags *and* butts. He gave me the once over and a confident tail wag okay. We chatted briefly on the recent introduction of two new flavours to Pedigree Chum's already extensive portfolio and then I was on my way. I had landed at Hobart airport, capital of Tasmania, and Mel was there to meet me. We embraced like we had known each other longer than we did and I realised, in the world of the backpacker, friendships are forged at a quicker pace, but this doesn't make them any less solid.

"Perfect timing," Mel beamed, "The Taste of Tasmania festival starts today. The luck of the Irish I suppose."

"Luck," I retorted, "I'm Irish. I know when there's a festival with opportune moments to drink too much."

"We'll head straight there so," she laughed.

The festival took place in a large warehouse by the docks made even larger by a marquee extension. It seemed the entire Tasmanian population was present, enjoying food and drink in unequal amounts. I was told it takes place every year to correspond with the famous Sydney to Hobart yacht race, where presumably they're racing to get to the bar first. Looking around, I would have had difficulty identifying the winners as most were happily drunk. We spotted Malcolm, the boys, Mel's friend Lisa and drinks waiting to be drunk. I settled into the warm community feeling as the night's entertainment got under way.

To my delight a juggler was first to take to the stage. I had spent my final year in school learning juggling tricks rather than the ins and outs of a worm's anatomy, or anything else that could have come up in the final exams for that matter, so I considered myself fairly good, maybe even a clown in the making some day if I was lucky. The next 20 minutes made me realise I was rubbish. With the skill of someone possessing a God-given talent the juggler had the large audience spellbound almost immediately. While juggling five batons non stop he was able to slip out of his suit jacket and trousers and then dress himself again, all the time to the beat of the accompanying music and without dropping one. His performance continued to include batons set on fire and pressure activated sound pads. Simply, he was in a league of his own. When the festivities died down Mel dropped me to a hostel I had booked from Sydney. She wasn't happy with me for doing this but I didn't want to be too presumptuous when it came to her hospitality. I was very wrong though and promised to join her family the following morning.

I moved the light curtain to one side. Through the window a working day in Hobart had begun, but there was no rush or obvious stress, all was relaxed, calm and bathed in glorious sunlight. Mel was already outside waiting for me, but before she showed me my new home it was time to see Hobart from an aerial view at the top of Mount Wellington which overlooks the city. We twisted our way upwards through trees on either side until we reached the mountain's bald peak and a view of the city that extended out over the water. It had become more common in recent years for those with money to relocate here from the everyday chaos Sydney can become, opting to avail of the short flight to and from their office instead. Already I could see why. The air was fresher, the people friendlier and the modern time restraints we impose on ourselves didn't seem to exist here to assist in one's stressful death. Yeah, I liked it. I suppose this is what drew me to Mel and Malcolm, the environment having direct impact on the person. I sensed no traffic-induced road rage, no deadlines missed punishable by death and no high blood-pressured problems to solve. They were just happy people, enjoying life, and as I was experiencing, very friendly and hospitable. It occurred to me right then that this was the problem with people back home, the insecurities, the unfriendliness, brought on by the environment we had created, consumed in greed. I noticed Mel looking at me weirdly so I took my camera out and froze her in a digital box.

We returned the same route we had arrived but at the bottom of the mountain we turned off for Mel's house. I was shown my room, my own double bed. After months in hostel dorm bunks and single beds, this was like checking into the Ritz. Mel handed me two sets of keys, one for the house and one for her Jeep. Slightly embarrassed by her trusting nature I knew it was my Irish nature kicking in. She waved it off and announced it was time to visit her friends, just down the road.

When we got there we were greeted at the door by Bob. After already spending over a month in Australia I can confidently say what stood in front of me now was the most typically stereotyped Ozzie I'd met. His string vest covered his pot belly but probably wouldn't in a month, or even after dinner. In one hand a can of beer swished from side to side, the other held a barbecue prongs dripping grease, the floor being saved a stain by his aforementioned belly. When he talked, it was from the side of his mouth and I couldn't understand a single word. Despite the language barrier though, I could tell I was more than welcome and gratefully accepted a beer, hoping our drunken language would meet somewhere in the middle of slurred comprehension a bit later. After a fantastic dinner and plenty more drink, it was time for a swim in their indoor pool, as you do.

The next day Malcolm brought me out on the boat he had told me about in Vietnam. He seemed quite excited about his yacht, as was I, and keen for me to see it. We made a quick stop at the yacht club to stock up on cold beers and it wasn't long before the anchor was lifted and we were leaving the harbour behind. We passed the boat that had won the Sydney to Hobart race, still anchored by the docks with no sign of life on board. Maybe the crew were recuperating on drips since the mammoth after party, looking forward to next year. We passed under the bridge that I'd arrived over coming from the airport. Malcolm explained that in 1975 a cargo ship collided with the Tasmin Bridge resulting in a number of deaths both on board the ship and of motorists crossing at the time. A local businessman was quick to start a ferry service though, ferrying thousands from the central business district of Hobart to the eastern shore, going on to make his fortune in ship building.

Still we sailed on, sandwiches and beers. As we hugged the coastline, the casino came into view. In the grounds a wedding was taking place. A possible gamble on a new life with a wife that had certainly taken a gamble on her wedding dress. I'll drink to that. Soon after we tacked. Malcolm did something with the jib. Ropes and pulleys worked together and the piece of wood at the back was pushed to one side. I'm not altogether au fait with boating terms, believe it or not, but the result was we were now headed back to the harbour.

Lisa was there to meet me so I removed my sea legs and adopted the ones for general everyday use. She looked at me strangely so I also removed my pirate hat, eye patch and fake hook, said one last 'aaarrrrr' and we were on our way. Thinking it was a good idea to lay off the drink, for a couple of hours anyway, we made for the cinema. Lisa had very kindly booked ahead and soon we were sitting in what looked like a very plush hotel reception ordering a three course meal and an accompanying bottle of red wine.

"Oh, so we're having dinner first then?" I cleverly observed.

"No, no," she smiled, "this is for the cinema."

"Eh, what happened to popcorn and coke?"

With that hanging in the air, our waitress inquired, "would you like your meal at the start, middle or end of the movie?"

"Middle is fine," Lisa replied, as I looked on.

We were shown to our seats which are better described as beds and I thought to myself if this was a date I'd be doing pretty well. Situated in twos, with a small table in the middle, the cinema sat about 50 in total. Throughout the film the waiting staff took on the personas of ninjas, skilfully delivering food and wine, never causing a distraction from the big budget Hollywood blockbuster. Such a good job, that food would seem to appear from nowhere on our table, and so enthralled by the movie, I wouldn't even remember eating it. By the time the end credits rolled, I was discovering the delights of Death.. by chocolate.

We decided we had room enough for a cocktail so made our way to the casino I had spotted earlier that day. It is the tallest building by far in Hobart. Its circular structure reminded me more of a government building which I thought was appropriate since they also like to take your hard earned money, claim to care and look in the opposite direction pretending it's nothing to do with them as you end up in the gutter. Have I said too much? The circular bar gave me the impression I was part of a small cog now turning the bigger wheel. I am sure the singing lounge lizard replaced a lyric in American Pie. 'Get them drunk and they will gamble.' I looked around and no one else seemed to have noticed. The barman smiled and was generous with his measures. I liked that.

Ben from Scotland, whom I'd met on the east coast conveyor belt, had also become bored and wanted something different, so he caught a flight to Hobart. When we had first met I had difficulty understanding his thick Scottish accent. He soon learnt to slow down his speech when meeting new people but once I was up to speed he didn't care – I could act as translator. We met in a backpacker's hangout, a cheap coffee house that doubled as an internet café. It was good to see him again. A plan was soon hatched and researched on the web. We'd rent a car and drive around Tasmania. We figured we had about a week to do it, taking into account time restraints due to impending flights and, of course, money. Our meeting moved on to an Irish bar around the corner and as we toasted the forthcoming adventure we agreed two more people would be ideal to share the experience, the cost, and the blame. Ideally women. By the time I'd been to the toilet, washed my hands, denied I was going grey in the mirror (just blonder), dried my hands and returned to our table, Ben had met, invited and was now planning with two excited girls. I first made sure they completely understood he wasn't giving away free prizes because it was a Scottish holiday, that in fact they had agreed to be encased in a small car for most of a week with Ben and me. That cleared up, they were disappointed there were no free gifts but then we cleverly got them drunk and they agreed to make the trip with us anyway.

Before I took off gallivanting around their island, Mel and Malcolm had plans for me. Keen lifeguards, like most of their friends, they loved to race the lifeguard boats. Nowadays these boats have been replaced with jet skis and dinghys to assist those in difficulty. But instead of fading out of fashion, the old boats have been redesigned for speed and carbon fibre-manufactured for, well, more speed. Teams are recruited yearly and tournaments fiercely fought anywhere there's a beach. They start in the shallow of the water, jump in on the mark and row like the clappers straight out to sea, over the ever growing waves. When a certain point is reached they return to the beach. It was pretty impressive to look at, four people pushing and pulling the large oars while one stood at the back, keeping balance while steering. This was a training day for them in preparation for an upcoming race. Men and women of all ages made up the 30 hopefuls to make a team, training together but on the day in separate categories.

They seemed to be doing well, only one boat capsizing so far and apparently it's easily done. Malcolm then shouted in my direction, "come on, it's your turn." I looked around but there was no one behind me. When I looked back it seemed training had finished and the small crowd were beckoning me over. I joined them, determined to give it my best shot.

"Right mate, you have to get changed first," Mel smiled.

"Ah, I'm grand, I'm wearing shorts I always swim in," I tried.

Mel produced something from behind her back and laughed with the rest.

"You gotta wear these mate."

Dangling from her hand was a black pair of speedos. I didn't like where this was going. I was going to be peer pressured into wearing budgie smugglers. Oh why could it not have been something normal like smoking? I had to quickly come to terms with the loss of dignity. There was nowhere to get changed and what I was putting on was hardly dignified anyway, closer to illegal. To roars of laughter I donned the de-dignifiers. "That's it, laugh at the Irishman," I quipped.

I looked ridiculous. My tanned legs stopped halfway up my thigh where Irish milk bottle white continued. I was just glad no one had a camera. Then, click, click. Click, click, click. Ah here, where did they have those? They're wearing speedos too. Did the new version of speedos come with hidden pockets and a built in GPS system now? I made for the water, thinking speedos should be in their natural habitat, but was once again stopped by Mel.

"One more thing," she managed through her laughter, "you have to push the back of your speedos into the crack of your arse."

"You're joking," I said deadpan.

"No, it's so your ass can slide easily on the seat while you row."

"You're loving this Mel, aren't you?"

Dignity dropped to a level I thought I'd never reach, I walked to the boat through Ozzie hysterics. Malcolm stood at the end of the boat with a huge grin on his face.

"Are you ready mate? You're rowing with the girls' team."

"What? This day can't get any lower."

But it did. It turned out I was particularly bad at rowing too. I tried to keep tempo with the girl beside me but as the waves increased in size, the oar got heavier, my arms got weaker and my ass was getting less hairy with each stroke. Malcolm did his best to put me off too.

"Don't get trapped under your oar if we capsize mate, that wouldn't be good," he shouted at me over the crashing of waves.

"I can't die in speedos," I shouted.

The girls laughed.

Tasmanian Surf Team 42   Embarrassed Irishman 1

Breathlessly we made it back to the beach and I stylishly fell out of the boat. A round of applause seemed to conclude their entertainment for the day. Bob slapped me on the back and said something, of which I hadn't a clue, so if in doubt I decided, mention the bar. He seemed more than happy with this response and proved he could move pretty quickly when he wanted to. I turned to Mel.

"Thanks for this, I'm glad I could give something back to the community while I'm here."

"A hairy Irish ass?" she smiled.

"No, I provide entertainment, and besides, it's just an Irish ass now thank you."

Road Trip

A map of Tasmania was spread out on the table before us. Mel was armed with a luminous pink marker, eager to highlight the best route we should take to make the most out of our limited time on the road. Clockwise, she made her way around the map, not that there is a lot of choice when it comes to roads here. She circled the 'must see' places and handed me a list of possible places to stay on the route, phone numbers included. I raided her CD collection, left to pick up the car and reminded myself to collect the others.

Maeve was the first Irish person I'd met in Tasmania after being surrounded by them on the mainland, and together with her German friend Sandra, they combined with myself and Ben to squeeze into our small but cheap motor. It didn't take us long to get lost, lose the map, get hungry, stop for lunch and eventually find the map and our way out of Hobart, but once we did, it was on perfect paved roads we travelled. Life on the highway mirrored the relaxed way of life in the city and we excitedly chatted the carefree miles away. The roads and scenery didn't resemble what I had experienced through my Greyhound window. Here, the road wouldn't stay straight for too long and a turn of a corner would see a change from Australian bush to a very familiar Irish countryside setting with fields full of sheep. The miles also seemed to eat away at our phones reception bar like pacman, until the only purpose they served was to tell the time.

The Central Highlands area of Tasmania is dominated by the Cradle Mountain – Lake St Clair National Park. With a depth of 200m, Lake St Clair is Australia's deepest lake and we made this our first stop. With ice creams bought, we sat on the cement pier that cut into the water. Forested mountains surrounded the lake and at the far side of the park we knew Cradle Mountain was there for us the next day. A small group passed us, decked out in all the hiking gear they'd need, rucksacks and tents on their backs. They would spend the next few days and nights making their way through the National Park also heading to Cradle Mountain. We breathed in the warm fresh air and returned to our car.

Continuing west, the road climbed higher, slicing a path straight through the centre of the Park. As we came to the far side the forest dispersed and we snaked our way on a narrow road into a valley down to an old mining town called Queenstown. Ghosts of past years told tales of money made and spent but, since the mining industry took a hit here, the town had lost its soul. The Royal Arms Hotel stood as the town's centrepiece. Once a youthful beauty queen, it had fallen from grace and now looked needy. Fights had become so common in the bar it was now known as the 'Swinging Arms'. Nothing to see here, keep moving.

We turned off the main road and cruised towards the ocean. Mel had recommended Strahan, a quiet picturesque fishing village, so we decided to spend our first night there. We located a hostel, parked the car and walked into town. The police station looked like a doll's house, a window each side of the door, a sign saying it was closed. We walked along the shoreline as the setting sun glistened over the water. The shine off each ripple made me blink the light away. There was one bar in the town of one street and the out-dated music kept us entertained with a drink before we made our way through the warm darkness to our beds.

We rose early and reloaded the car, knowing there was a long day ahead of us. To stick to the schedule there were miles to be covered. We rejoined the main road and headed north, running parallel to the National Park. By lunch we entered it once again, this time on the Cradle Mountain side. We stopped at the visitor's centre for something to eat, checked out the price of the helicopter ride we wished we could afford, then caught the tourist bus to Dove Lake. Cradle Mountain towered over the water and as we trekked through the neighbouring forest we realised how the mountain got its name. From the right angle the summit takes the shape of a baby's head lying in its cradle, peacefully sleeping, probably due to all the fresh air it's getting up there. After trekking for the afternoon we returned to the car and made our way to Burnie on Tasmania's north shore. This time our accommodation was situated over a bar. With its tightly packed rooms and narrow corridors, Ben compared it to a scene from Resident Evil, all we were missing were the zombies.

After an uneventful night that meant we were all still among the living, we drove along the coast road to Launceston, Tasmania's second biggest city. The contrast between here and our previous night's stay was evident in large shopping centres, chain coffee shops, modern bars, a sizeable college campus and a Burger King. We settled into our room, this time above an Irish bar, and went in search of free internet access in the local library. Due to the existence of the college, there are a lot of young people living here and, as Friday aged into the evening, the Irish bar became their lecture hall. A live band had set up in the corner and in the beer garden a DJ bounced beats off the

walls and into the clear night sky. I stood in the doorway between both and got rocked hip hop style. Ben suggested Jaeger
Bombers and proposed since we were staying upstairs, the money we saved on a taxi could be spent at the bar. It's funny, the
excuses we can make up after a few drinks just to have a few
more. Maybe we're all borderline alcoholics, just some of us
have forgotten our passports.

As the hangovers hit, headaches were passed around the car
like an infectious outbreak of the 'flu. Breakfast was water and
painkillers but today's drive wasn't too far. Our destination was
close to St. Helen's, the northernmost town on the East coast.
Not far from there, in a town called Scamader, I had arranged
to met Mel and Malcolm. Their team was competing in a surf
boat race that day and I was a bit surprised after my debut that
I wasn't asked to help out. Just outside the town we stopped at
the 'Pub in the Paddock' for much needed coffee and toasted
sandwiches. Unfortunately we missed the boat race but arrived
on time for the drinks reception which none of us could handle.
We sipped beers and daydreamed of bed.

We made an early start the next day and decided we'd wait to
have breakfast, again on Mel's recommendation, at the mouth
watering sounding 'Pancake Barn'. A turn off the main road
found us in the middle of nowhere and just as our will and
our stomachs were about to concede defeat, a large house came
into view. The quiet of the morning was done away with as we
opened the door to a full house of ordering and eating. I had
no idea where all the people had come from but agreed with
their choice of eatery after sampling a delicious chicken and
mushroom pancake. We were set up for the day, as they say, but
really just until lunch when we'd be hungry again.

Our next stop was Wine Glass Bay, one of the most popular
tourist spots here. We parked in the designated car park and set
out on the wooded trail that would take us there. The pace was
slow going under the midday's blazing sun. As we started to de-

scend, the beach came into view, with all those who had made it there before us. The beach followed the perfect curve of a wine glass, its contents a strong blue liquid topped off with soft white sand and sprinkled with people. I don't think it's a drink that would take off in the common market, mainly due to cannibalism being illegal and all that, but it was beautiful to look at. To be a part of. We trekked back to the car after a time and drove on to Swansea, a little further down the coast. A modern hostel greeted our tired bones and a local restaurant lined our stomachs before our eyes decided to stay shut.

We awoke to our last day on the road and as we gained ground on Hobart we all agreed on what a great few days we had had. The Tasmanian people themselves seem to have to put up with a lot of stick from those on the mainland, in the same vein Kerrymen or Northsiders do here. Abuse on a wide range of topics from being stupid to being inbred, I suppose one could lead to the other, whatever order you choose. On the local radio now, a story I thought at first was a joke. A Tasmanian brother and sister, separated at birth, had got married and were several months into marital bliss before the truth raised its deformed head. They were in the process of suing whoever they could sue and I presume dividing their belongings and moving into separate places. This wasn't the vast expanse of America, the land of Jerry Springer, this was Tasmania, and with a population of less than half a million, it was a little hard to believe. In the car though, we had already made up our minds about the people here, so we just laughed it off and drove on.

We dropped the girls off at their hostel and the car back to the garage. I said goodbye to Ben but knew I'd be seeing him soon in Melbourne, and returned to my home away from home. As Mel prepared another fabulous meal for us I told her I had to catch a flight the following day. I saw the same look of disappointment on her face that I felt in my stomach.

"We could sort out a job for you, there's no problem with you staying here."

"I know Mel, thanks for everything, really, I don't want to go, but there's flights I have to make."

That night's dinner was slightly more downbeat. I kept thinking to myself about staying, while all the talk was about where I was going next. I said goodbye to Malcolm and the boys, and Mel insisted on driving me to the airport early the following morning.

My teeth were sore when I awoke, I had been grinding them in my sleep. My subconscious telling me something wasn't quite right? Maybe. Little was said on the road to the airport.

"Mel, have you heard why Aborigines never say goodbye?" I asked.

"Why's that?"

"Because they don't believe in them, they believe you'll always meet again. I like that idea."

"So do I," Mel replied softly.

We hugged tight, then tighter. There wasn't much left to say, I'd said my thank you's ad nauseam. I threw my rucksack over one shoulder, smiled and said, "Farewell."

Melbourne

A heatwave had engulfed Melbourne as I arrived, and my melting rucksack seemed even heavier. I found a bus outside the airport that would drop me to St. Kilda, where I had booked my next hostel. On the way there I received a very welcome text from Lee in Sydney.

"Fuck a job, I'm coming down to Melbourne."

I cleverly deciphered from the one line message that Lee was holding off looking for work and instead was going to join me for some more drunkenness. I liked his career choice and confirmed he'd be arriving in a couple of days.

The hostel was modern in its appearance and way of thinking. It seemed newly built and adhered to the idea of cramming as many people as possible into small spaces. Like apartment blocks these days, the units have shrunk in size but have, in turn, grown in numbers. All that's missing is the suspended water bottle, a running wheel and the floor covered in straw. My dual bunk bed room felt like being placed inside a snow globe so I headed out.

St. Kilda is the arty area of Melbourne. The lives of musicians, actors, artists and backpackers combine here and the best place to experience this is in the famous Espy. A friend back home had told me about this place, right down to what band would be playing each night, and she had left Melbourne a few years previously. This slow-paced easygoing way of life was particularly suited to here. The Espy itself, a beach front hotel, didn't seem to have been touched by either paint or screwdriver in the passing years. As had been predicted, the same bands were on. Three bars gave you three different types of music, from gospel right through to rock and punk. I loved it.

As promised, I had kept in touch with a couple of girls from Melbourne whom I had met on my night camping on The Beach. On that one perfect night I must have been firing on all cylinders, and had them in stitches of laughter. Convinced I was actually a comedian back home, they were eager to bring me to stand-up comedy night in the city with a group of their friends. I was delighted to see them again but I started to get an inkling that they had built me up as some sort of comic genius to their friends. They seemed to be waiting for me to hit them with some killer one-liners. After a quick drink we moved on to the comedy club. The following three acts were not the forte of up and coming Australian comedy and in-between terrible jokes I could hear my friend whisper, 'John would be much better up there.' Fortunately the opportune moment never arose to make a fool of myself and by the time we'd left the club her friends had no longer an interest in comedy. If I had to listen to those comedians again, I would no longer have an interest in living.

Lee arrived the next day so we booked into the same hostel in the city. The grid-shaped streets make it easy to negotiate your way around the familiar sounding street names. I told Lee the story about the Australian girl who had offered me free passage here years before. He agreed I had to at least let her know I'd eventually made it. I found an internet café and sent off a short message which included my phone number. As we left to find some place to eat, my phone rang.

"Hi, it's Jill."

The conversation seemed slightly surreal, like it was a past exchange but only happening now. We agreed to meet for coffee in a couple of days' time. Catch up, start again, stay strangers, who knew?

That night we checked out O'Reillys Irish Bar by the river and with the arrival of more friends from the road, the drinks flowed. The live band seemed to spur on the drinking, as we caught up on where the last few weeks had taken us. I seemed to take on board more shots than I could swallow and had just registered the room was spinning when I got a tap on the shoulder.

"John, it is you."

I turned to face Jill. The eight years weren't enough to fade our familiarity from memory. I was excited to see her but realised this was a bad time for a surprise reunion considering my previous two hours drinking.

"Yeah, I made it," I managed.

We disappeared into the background, away from the band's enthusiastic performance, found a table and caught up on the years past. I really loved Melbourne and wondered where my life would have been if I had accepted her invite all those years before.

It was tennis time here with the Australian Open already in full flight. During the day, Confederation Square was packed with enthusiasts basking in the sun while watching a game on the outdoor big screen. $25 gained you entry into the stadium itself, so I followed the crowds down Batman Avenue (I love it!)

the following morning. I entered into an open grassy area that was overlooked by the Rod Laver Arena, the main stadium, and surrounded by bars and food stalls. In the corner a stage had been set up and that day's featured artists were well on the way to entertaining the crowd that were also taking in the day's tennis action on the big screen. I gravitated towards the live music and allowed myself to be sucked into the world of unknown up and comings wishing for their big break. As the day drew on I realised I hadn't seen any live tennis yet and it was the Australian Open after all, not an outdoor music festival. I crossed over to one of the accessible courts for those who had paid as little as me and found the Williams sisters doing a very believable impersonation of brothers trouncing a petite female pairing.

Satisfied I'd taken in at least one major sporting event I returned via the Bat Avenue to the city. Lee and myself once again departed. He had a job hunt to undertake back in Sydney and soon I'd be leaving Australia behind. I loved the idea of keeping in touch with people I'd met along the way with the hope of enjoying a reunion at some stage. Small familiarities on a road of unknowns. Kevin was one half of the couple I'd shared a few days with and had also endured the red cocktails on Paradise Island. Originally from Ireland, he had long since become resident in Melbourne and had done very well in his working life. His family home was in the quiet countryside, so during his working week in the city he stayed in his apartment in the Eureka Building. At 300m, it was the world's tallest residential tower at the time when measured to its highest floor and after dinner I got to take in the impressive view of the sprawling city in front of me. 46 storeys below, the Yarra river made its way past the Crown Casino and to my right I could see the tennis ground I had visited earlier that day.

This was my last night in Australia, a country that both frustrated me and gave birth to a deep down urge to stay. A champagne cork popped as we toasted to paths being crossed and the friendliness in strangers. I tilted my glass and took in my final gaze of the city's lights. Happy just to be there, that I'd finally made it, even if my copy of 'The rough guide to Melbourne' was ridiculously out of date.

Chapter 9

PASTRY PURSUIT

South Island

My plan was to drive around New Zealand. I could enjoy my own time-tableless freedom, avoiding the restrictions which are placed on you by using public transport. My budget wouldn't allow me to do this on my own though, besides, a solitary road trip is about as much fun as learning the rules of cricket, so I arranged to meet two friends. Irish Rossi would meet me in Melbourne airport, whereas English Brownie was already awaiting our arrival in a hostel in Christchurch. The short flight went as the captain planned, without engine failure resulting in the death of everyone on board, and when we disembarked we were glad to see our luggage had made the trip too. As we walked through arrivals a young girl ran up to Rossi.

"Hiya uncle," she excitedly said through a broad smile.

"Okay," was all Rossi managed, taken aback.

Not getting the enthusiasm, or the present she had expected, she turned to her mother who was embarrassingly signalling at her, her wrong choice of relative. She retreated as quickly, leaving a bemused and slightly embarrassed look on Rossi's face.

"Damn it," I said, "I thought we were going to get a free lift into town, come on, let's find the bus."

We checked into our hostel that faced an old Gothic Church, and was informed our friend was in the bar, getting to know it intimately. It was great to see Brownie again, our paths had crossed for the first time in Asia and we had subsequently travelled through many towns together. He had made me laugh continuously with stories of his friends back home that appeared in my head as characters out of an episode of 'Little Britain'. He had a sense of humour, ideal to this road trip party.

After a night's sleep, we set out to explore Christchurch, and to sort out our would-be road trip transportation. While travelling I loved the extremes of my ever changing surroundings. Like leaving the Mongolian Steppe for language barrier bedlam Beijing or the hazy valleys of outback Nimbin to the strip club circus of Sydney's Kings Cross. I had now, it seemed, gone from a laid back city to a laid back town. Pedestrianised streets and squares were coloured with street performers and buskers. People stopped and listened, forming a crowd of carefree sign ups. The sun did its job for the performance, taking care of the vast theatre's stage lighting and auditorium heating.

We made our way from act to act like we had been sent from afar to judge, before our noses picked up a scent and our mouths watered. New Zealand is famous for its pies. With great imagination, ingredients are combined and freshly cooked each morning, and for as little as NZ$3 you can have any one of your daily meals looked after. As I bit into my choice of chicken and mushroom, the warm sauce mixing perfectly with the dryness of the pastry, I foresaw my coming weeks' diet and how budget friendly it was. I had just finished a book about a Kiwi guy who had cycled from London to Christchurch because he'd missed these beloved pies. Although extreme, I could certainly see his point now, 'A long way to go for pie' indeed – but worth it. Never again would I brave an overheated Spar pie at three in the morning to try to combat the hunger several pints had brought on. Imposters, I tells you, imposters.

After a couple of hours of bad tennis in the park, constantly checking our racquets for holes, we located and booked our next few weeks' all-in-one accommodation and transport. Known as a Spaceship, our bright orange and white people carrier was named Sith. It turned out all the Spaceships had a Star Wars themed name, as we'd notice in the coming days, passing each other on the road and sharing the same camp-sites. Sith comfortably slept two people, when one was me and the other a gorgeous blonde female, unfortunately neither Rossi nor Brownie fit that description so we took it in turns to sleep in the tent we'd also rented. Besides that, it was well equipped with a fridge, gas cooker, DVD player, storage and foldaway table and chairs. The real clincher came in the price, at NZ$70 a day, it was the cheapest way to drive around the country. We consulted the map that was provided, agreed on a route (much like Tasmania, there wasn't a huge choice when it came to roads) and headed south to the town of Dunedin.

We could all drive, so taking turns in concentrating wasn't a problem. En route we stocked up on emergency supplies. Food for those times a pie shop couldn't be located and of course drink to drown our sorrows of being pieless. A few hours under our fan belt, we made it to our destination beach side town and drove straight out the other side. It didn't seem to hold the delights Christchurch had displayed and gave off a work rather than play aura to us. We found a sandy camp site and made use of our table and chairs and a pack of cards for the night, easily settling into the carefree simplicities of a road trip.

After a morning spent aiming Frisbees at each other's heads on the beach, we packed up and headed inland and north to Queenstown. Here a picturesque town has been transformed into an extreme sports funderland for backpackers. During the winter, the imposing mountains that rise from the town are snow covered, catering for skiers and boarders alike. Now in the heat of the summer, white water rafting, luging (gravity propelled engineless go-karts), bungy jumping and sky diving took over the menu. The small town also boasts the now world renowned Fergburger, which itself can boast having queues longer than any at the bars at the end of the night, as the thirsty get hungry. As well as those treats, The Earth Bar supplies cocktails in teapots, a novel if not ridiculous way to get pissed. I had my heart set on doing a sky dive but had been advised on where I should do it, so after a couple of days we continued on the road, north.

Our next stop was top of my list to see in New Zealand. The small lakeside town Te Anau was where my other sister had been a few years back. The photograph she had taken, framed and given to me as a house warming present had urged me to finally get on a plane and leave Ireland. I had long since wanted to retake the photograph with myself centre stage, proof that I'd made it here or I dare say, that anything is possible. The lake appeared before the town, the same mountains on the far side matching exactly my photograph, daring nature to even try to change them. I spotted the small wooden pier and turned Sith off the road down a stony decline. I got out and walked towards the lake, thinking of all the times the pier in the photograph had previously teased me to step onto it, when I couldn't. It seemed to always know when I was at my lowest points in life so it was funny now as I reached it, it had me on a high. I slowly stepped onto the pier and started to walk along it, trying to memorise each wooden plank as I passed over it and the glimpse of water between each. At the end I stopped, breathed in the fresh air coming off the lake through a smile to match the mountains in size and turned for a photograph.

We had still a long drive ahead of us but there was enough time to find the local pie eatery for some pie time. We were driving on what was conceivably a very long cul de sac towards Milford Sounds. After our sight seeing was done we'd have to return to Queenstown in order to take a different road out of the town to continue north. The light was failing as we reached the end of the road and there was little else for us to do but to find accommodation or, as was the case tonight, set up camp. We had spent the previous nights in camp sites where kitchen and toilet facilities were gratefully used, so it was time to rough it at the side of the road. We had passed a small inlay close to the road end and thought this would be suitable. Unfortunately the midgets also saw it as a suitable hang out spot and thwarted us as we attempted to light a fire. Rain earlier in the day had dampened any available wood so clothes we could afford to sacrifice were set alight but the returning rain saw to it that it was futile. We retreated to Sith to escape the rain and midgets, both now invisible in the darkness. We tentatively used the gas stove inside and cooked a feast of mashed potatoes from a packet, and rashers, the whole thing generously covered in tomato ketchup. Dessert was a couple of cookies. We wouldn't have traded it right then for a Michelin Star Restaurant, we couldn't have been happier.

The night's rain had lifted leaving behind a warm dampness to our tent and surrounding area the next morning. We travelled the short distance once again to the end of the road and purchased the early morning boat tickets that would show us why Milford Sounds was so popular. A light breakfast was waiting for us on board and we ate as the boat left its moorings. Huge mountains and cliffs on both sides looked down on us and the dead calm water we glided through. At regular intervals fresh springs seemed to appear from solid rock and follow the sharp mountainous contours to add to the water level below. Although the rain had ceased, the remaining misty cloud covered the cliff peaks at positions decided on by the wind, giving it a very eerie but peaceful feel from our lowly viewpoint. I could see why New Zealand was used as the location for 'The Lord of the Rings' trilogy. There was both a mystical and magical feel to our surroundings, like we were in the centre of a crystal ball, slowly encroaching on the future. Before the tunnel of water joined the vast ocean we turned and retreated from whence we came.

Leaving the water, we returned to the road and spent the rest of the day driving back to Queenstown, resisted temptation to stop and continued on to Wanaka. It was late when we arrived so we found a camp site and slept while Sith's engine cooled. The next morning the brilliant sun had already started work, heating the inside of my tent until I eventually woke in a sweat. I gave in to being awake and joined the lads for breakfast. Wanaka is another town that has emerged beside a lake. It seemed Kiwis certainly love water. We discovered on one side of the lake there was a winery. New Zealand wine has fast become one of the most popular in the world, many agreeing their crisp, fruity Sauvignon Blancs can't be matched. The interesting thing about this particular winery was that some of its land was dedicated to a game we weren't familiar with: Golf Cross.

We made our way on a narrow road, cutting through the growing vines either side, and eventually dropping down towards the lake we arrived at the small winery that doubled as the clubhouse. We were each given a score card (that also explained the rules on the back) clubs, oval golf balls and unusual cone-shaped tees. Golf Cross seemed to be a cross between golf and American football. Instead of aiming for a flag on a carefully groomed green, we would be firing our oval shaped balls towards scaled down American football posts. Before each shot you had to tee up the ball on the special coned tees and then hope to hear the unusual whirr sound which meant you'd connected accurately. Because of the shape of the ball though, the distance it covered in the air was nothing compared to that of a normal golf ball, so progress was slow in the sweltering heat.

After tasting the winery's other delights we left Wanaka. We twisted our way on a cliff top coastal road and watched as the sea and land met with a crash of white foamy spray over the jagged rocks below. It was so beautiful none of us wanted to drive, preferring instead to marvel at nature's postcard. Soon after, the road turned inland and climbed over the mountains. Thick green forests spread out above and below us like an artist had spent years painting perfection, each tree seemed correctly positioned and coloured. By late evening we arrived in Nelson. Although we were spending hours on the road, the scenery we were experiencing made it enjoyable. After a pie fix in the town, we settled into our camp site. We had all managed a few hours' sleep before we were woken by a thunderous roar as Sith shook on its wheels. We were camped directly under a cargo plane's flightpath and we soon became aware there was a whole fleet of them. Luckily today was a day we needed to be up early. We had to drive to Picton and catch the car ferry to Wellington, leaving the south island behind for New Zealand's other half. On the way I discovered a breakfast pie; egg, beans and bacon enclosed in a pastry dome. It seemed to sum up my Kiwi adventure so far. A balanced mix of ingredients at the perfect temperature, encased to keep in the flavour and keep out the harsh realities. There was but one word – yum.

North Island

The ferry crossing was relaxed. We had lunch and played cards. Across the water, Wellington awaited us. We decided to spend the weekend there and had timed it well as the Rugby 7s final was taking place. Kiwis are fanatical about their rugby so we were guaranteed a party. When the ferry docked we brought Sith back to life and followed the directions in our guidebook to the camp site. Unfortunately it was further out of the city than we thought, so we'd have to rely on public transport for the weekend.

That evening the weekend party kicked off. When we made it into the city, it appeared everyone had made a huge effort to win an imaginary fancy dress competition. The bars were overflowing with costumes both skilfully made and bought. The atmosphere was excitable and contagious and soon we were in the thick of it. In the time I'd already spent in the country, I had taken to the people. Compared to the Australians, they seemed friendlier, less brash and more inclined to take an interest in you and help out. Maybe the amount of Irish here hadn't yet reached saturation point unlike, I felt, across the water. As we explained to a group of locals how we had come to be here, they inquired as to where we were staying. Hearing the result and disappointed in the distance we'd have to travel on public transport, they immediately offered us a place to stay in the city the following night. It cemented my high opinion of the Kiwis.

The following day, relaxing in the camp site, we tuned into the Rugby 7s on Sith's radio. We were curious to hear if the All Blacks had won and would then know what to expect in the city that night. The New Zealanders' carefree sense of humour is evident even in their radio advertisements, verging on the risqué and no doubt unplayable in this part of the corporate world. The voice of the station's roving reporter in the stadium then broke the silence.

"There's a big problem down here," she reported with authority to the studio HQ, "I'm going to see what some of the crowd think about it."

With that, a certain Matt, at this stage very drunk, slurred to life across the nation's radio waves. He managed a couple of simple answers to the reporter's inquiries, before she hit him with some devastating news.

"I've just been told the stadium's bars have run out of alcohol, Matt, how'd you feel about that?"

A brief few seconds of silence followed as Matt gathered his thoughts and the question finally made sense through his head full of booze.

"Oh fuck," echoed over the airwaves. A slight shake of panic evident in his voice and a desperation that would be akin to hearing of the death of a loved one. Back in the studio laughing hysterics had started and another successful sound bite was completed. I thought about the same happening back home and how it would be followed by a vacant job position to be filled.

The All Blacks triumphed in the end, adding substance to their world domination and coal to the fire of the party atmosphere which went into overdrive. Live music leaked out onto the street from each packed bar and traffic stood still as the costumed occupants followed suit. No one seemed to mind though, as excitement had its firm grip on the city and attempts were made to drink it dry.

As the clean-up operation began the next morning and thousands of headaches kicked in, we slipped out the city's back door.

We found a Burger King to try to ease our own hangovers and then let Sith eat the miles we needed to cover that day. I had an uneasy feeling in my stomach that wasn't related to alcohol. A mixture of nerves and excitement was slowly growing greater and I knew why. Our next stop was Taupo, yet another lakeside haven, but this lake was my chosen one to see from a great height as I jumped out of a plane. It had been recommended to me by a girl I'd met in Cambodia and at the time I confidently promised to do it.

Taupo is built on a slight incline, each road making its way down to the large lake. At the top of one of these roads we found our camp site. When I expressed my interest in jumping out of a plane the elderly couple who ran the site were more than helpful in making the call and organising the whole thing.
"Tomorrow morning at nine, love," they said.
Right, now I just needed to sleep for the night.

Surprisingly I fell into a deep sleep or, as I liked to think, parachuted safely into it. Either way, the next morning I was refreshed and ready to go, not to mention nervous as hell and unable to eat. The bright yellow bus arrived from 'Taupo Tandem Skydiving' and I joined several others in tempting fate. The airfield wasn't far and our nervous chat ended so we could listen to our enthusiastic receptionist on arrival. Each of us were assigned a veteran skydiver to whom we'd be strapped while falling from the sky. I was introduced to Freddy, a crazy-looking Austrian wearing a horned helmet but as cool as a night in the Ice Hotel. A chart on the wall kept track of the instructors' jump totals. Freddy had completed 15,000 so far, I presumed all successful as he was now standing beside me talking about becoming the shape of a banana. I nodded my agreement, as if I was an expert in suitable fruit shapes to make while plummeting to the ground at freight train speeds, but couldn't help notice the other instructors repacking their parachutes, ready for another jump. As we walked out to the small plane that had taxied towards us, I just hoped Freddy was having a good 'parachute-packing day'.

I was the last one to take my seat on the floor of the plane and when I did it was full to capacity. Five eager students with their respective teachers. There was little room to manoeuvre once seated, which meant being last on, I'd be first out and quite obviously if I didn't go, no one else could. But there was no question of that happening, I felt a rush of determination and surprisingly quite fearless and calm. Freddy reassuringly talked into my ear sky diving facts, figures and anecdotes, as our small yellow plane climbed higher. Then a green light flashed on in front of us, we'd reached our required height and the door was opened. The view through it was breathtaking. The ground below looked like a patchwork quilt as we moved on towards the glass blue lake. There wasn't a cloud in the blue sky, nothing to impair our vision of the onrushing earth after we jumped.

"Swing your legs out John," I heard Freddy say in my ear. Without a second thought my legs were dangling over the side as I faced my soon to be new environment and I realised, although I'm afraid of heights, I wasn't scared. I think I was so high up it didn't really make sense to me, my brain slightly confused by distance. I felt Freddy's hand on my forehead, tucking my head into his shoulder, so I wouldn't accidentally break his nose or worse still, knock him out on exit. We rocked back and forth as he said the words; one, two, three and then my world turned upside down as we tumbled out of the plane. For a split second I caught sight of the door we had just left and noticed how fast we were moving away from it. Then Freddy spun me over so I was face down and I had to catch my breath as the water and land below us registered. Although we were falling at close to 120mph it didn't feel like it. It felt like we were flying as the on coming air cushioned our skin, just like holding your hand outside the car window as you drive. My senses were alive and my emotions ran riot. Adrenaline filled my body as my exhilarated mind tried to take it all in. Freddy tapped me on my shoulder just before he pulled the parachute chord and we jumped back into the sky. He loosened my harness slightly so I could get into a seating position as we floated peacefully towards the ground, the rush of wind in my ears now gone.

As we landed on the grass beside the airstrip I looked back and saw the others lining up to do the same. I stood up and felt alive. I wanted to go straight back up and jump again. We gathered together and took photos. This was a rush like no other. I thanked Freddy and then joined the awaiting bus of delighted students. Back at the camp site the couple were there to enquire about the morning's activity. Upon hearing all went well they said, " I suppose we can tell you this now."

"About six months ago a guy did his own skydive but his shoot didn't open. He landed in a bush though and was lucky to walk away with just two broken legs."

Interestingly put, I thought, but glad they had waited to tell me.

I was still very giddy so it was decided it was best if I didn't drive as we left Taupo. We made good time and before lunch we had reached Rotorua, a town that could do with some deodorant. The many geysers in this area gave off the constant smell of sulphites, mainly noticed by the visitors, as the locals had grown used to it. After our daily recommended pie intake we decided to play a game of golf on the local course. It proved quite tricky as the course was also built around geysers, a hazard you couldn't take a shot out of. When we finished up the round we chose to push on to Auckland where we could enjoy a night in a proper bed before we parted ways.

We parked Sith in the car park opposite and checked into the hostel. It had been a great few weeks and Sith stood up to its test of character. We hadn't done too badly either. Of course, spending all that time together and hours of continuous driving didn't pass without the odd argument. But the country we were travelling through and the people we were meeting gelled us together. After a great night's sleep, it was time to drop Brownie off at the airport, and then return Sith to his rightful owner or ruler, who knows. Brownie was off to the beaches of Fiji and, as we departed, I hoped it wouldn't be the last time I'd see him. The returning of Sith was less painful but I took a bright orange wrist band as a memento of our road trip. That just left myself and Rossi. We had a flight to LA to catch where we would then part ways. New Zealand had treated us well and had rejuvenated my travelling spirit after it had been slightly tampered with on Australia's east coast. A whole new continent was mine to explore tomorrow, my excitement already bubbling up like the beer I poured into my chilled glass on my last night in the land of the pie.

Chapter 10

BIG LIGHTS WILL INSPIRE YOU

LA

In a voice that seemed more suited to securing million dollar deals or safe passage for hostages, the pilot talked us through the plane's situation in its current airborne environment. "Sit back, relax, and I'll speak to you all later in the flight," his suave American drawl ended. A man who seemed confident of his own brilliance. The small screen facing me flickered to life as the cabin crew sprang into action upon hearing the 'bong' that indicated the lesser need for a fastened seatbelt. I switched through the available channels, trying to plot a path that would appear to quicken my time seated and ordered the chicken. An abrupt crackle was backed up by the return of the pilot's voice. "Everyone to their seats immediately."

The words hung, suspended for a few seconds, like they were unable to find somewhere to settle. His confidence no longer evident. The sentence spoken too quickly to be sure, but re-running it in your head you were certain there was a hint of panic. Beside me, Rossi let out a nervous laugh.

"This can't be good," he said, as the cabin crew dropped their food preparation as quickly as their smiles and belted up. We were flying from Auckland to LA, an area over the Pacific that is well known for turbulence. The plane shook from side to side as we braced ourselves for the presumed worst to come, but all fell silent save for the plane's powerful engines. When the pilot realised he'd over reacted, my chicken arrived as the first movie started.

When we landed, myself and Rossi made plans to meet up again and then said our goodbyes. I headed straight to Culver City where my auntie had offered me a place to stay for a few days. My flight leaving Auckland was an evening departure so I had spent the day taking in the last of the sights and relaxing in the cinema. Now, on a hot bright sunny day in LA, I stood once again in Thursday morning. Thanks to the time zones I was getting a second chance of living a day, before I'd lose it again closer to home. Or was it already one I was owed in lieu? Time was becoming as confusing as some of the currency rates I'd exchanged to and from, and I don't even wear a watch. I decided I'd text my sister to declare I had a day up on her and she responded quickly. "You don't look a day older!" Unfortunately, later that day I was caught. Just nicked by time, I suppose you could say, as my body succumbed to jet lag. I fell into a heavy sleep, waking occasionally just to start again.

When I was finally awake enough to focus, I was also awake enough to realise I was hungry. I was in the right country for a large appetite though, and took a seat in a nearby Denny's that specialises in breakfast. My plate was larger than any I'd previously used for a Sunday roast and it would take a lot of practice to wipe it clean. I tried my best and then decided on a walk by the ocean.

Santa Monica reminded me of home. Not caused by the streets, the beach, the pier or even the people. It was back at home where I'd seen numerous music videos and movies that now made the palm tree-lined streets so familiar. As I walked down the pier I felt it was already known to me. Stalls and musicians vied for the passing crowd's attention. Over the side, surfers patiently waited on their ticket to ride, while a path cutting through the sandy beach eased the course of rollerblades and bikes. Away from the sea, on a paved pedestrianised street, parallel to the palm trees, buskers entertained in the hope of shifting a few CDs. They were well organised, showing up with their own equipment, playing for their selected hour and then sticking around to support their fellow artists. I was amazed at the standard I was hearing. These were in a league far higher than the now seemingly standard Oasis covers buskers that dot their unimaginative way down Grafton Street. After a surprising set that contained both covers and originals, their $10 album seemed like a steal. As I made my way down the street, coffee in hand, my music collection expanded.

After a very chilled day it was time to catch a bus back to Culver. With the sun starting to dip in the distance, Santa Monica took on an unsettling appearance. Like Cinderella not making it home before midnight, the grassy area from which the palm trees sprung had transformed and was now choc a bloc with the homeless. Beauty had turned ugly. They faced expensive hotels and watched as luxury cars drove past. Something was very wrong with this picture. I was glad to see volunteers working their way through the sea of shopping trolleys offering blankets and sandwiches. Maybe, also, the small comfort that someone cares.

Another great night's sleep and I was back on public transport heading in the direction of Hollywood, where dreams became lives and reality mostly hit hard. On a packed bus, the open windows weren't enough to drop the temperature. Straight out of a miscast advert for Coca Cola, a large woman in rollerblades got on, singing loudly to a song only she could hear through her headphones. She sang and moved her way through her audience, the passengers, to take to her stage, the centre of the bus. Eyes averted in directions every which other way, feigning passiveness, as one would do when in the presence of a possible lunatic. But I couldn't avoid staring. A smile had commandeered my lips and it was taking all my will power to look away. This bizarre display of confidence or madness was proving hypnotic. I had heard that if you live in LA you really need a car. I presumed this was essential for the ease of getting around but maybe it was really for your own safety and sanity.

It took me two hours and a change to the underground to finally make it to Hollywood, not counting the previous months of planes, trains, buses and bikes, of course. An abundance of tourist buses had already beaten me and camera clicks became the common language amongst the swarming crowd. I watched as hand sizes were compared to those of the stars immortalised in cement. Excitement spread when a match was found and a dozen clicks held the evidence for back home. It would take a little more to excite me, possibly the discovery of a matching bank balance would do it. I kept walking, a sudden urge not to be among your average tourist. Further on I found an old diner and ordered what I hoped was a new hamburger. As I sat there I wondered had it been previously used for a movie. It certainly had character; like a very old, last standing Eddie Rockets, about to go out of business later that day with the final sale of a Classic and garlic fries. They say everyone here either has a script or the ability to act, just like everyone has a song written in Nashville. As my coffee was thrown, rather than poured, into my off white mug, I tried to typecast my old waitress. I decided the horror, science fiction side of the industry would best suit her, and a saving of make-up would at least be made.

A bar, I did know had featured in a movie, was a nice change of atmosphere after the diner dinner. Just off the main Hollywood strip I found the door for Boardner's which was in Johnny Depp's Ed Wood movie, a fantastic story of a not so talented cross dressing director. Not long into my first drink, conversation was shared with those seated at the bar. Two actors named some films they'd been in, which I'd never heard of, but surprisingly had no work lined up for this particular afternoon so a drink was in order. Closer to me, Dave had spent the last year surfing in Hawaii and was on his way home to New York. Closer still, from Orange County, Brian and Jessica were down here working on the roads. When asked my own story, Jessica looked a little perplexed.

"Where's Ireland?" she innocently asked.

"In Europe," I said with a smile.

"Where?" I had managed to confuse her even more, what was I thinking?

"You know England? Well beside it."

"Aahhh yeah," she registered, "I've just never been out of Orange County."

I'd heard of similar conversations before and although to us it's hard to believe, I had already travelled enough to understand how different lives can be. As we continued on to other bars her general friendliness made up for her limited knowledge of geography. I couldn't help comparing this to Irish women I'd met back home, and asked myself the question: which do I prefer? The well educated Irish girl who commonly lacks confidence to talk to a stranger and too easily gets suspicious if engaged in chat, or the happy go lucky friendly American who hasn't benefited from as good an education but exudes unashamed friendliness towards other people? Not much of a contest, I thought, as she set up the pool table for another game.

I was up early the next morning for a breakfast to beat that of Denny's. My auntie had filled the table with cereal, eggs, toast and juice. Nicely full, we said our goodbyes and I once again made my way into the city, but this time to leave it. A bus, train, bus combo would see me in San Francisco that night.

San Francisco

"Have you just arrived?" the girl sitting opposite asked.

I was in the city less than an hour and had already been lost, and after travelling for the day I imagined I wasn't the prettiest sight. I just hoped I was now on the correct tram.

"Yeah, I have, came from LA."

She spied my rucksack, the months in use now showing on the material.

"You been travelling for long then?"

"About seven months so far, I gather you've done the same?"

"Yeah," she smiled, "not long back after a year travelling, it's not easy being home!"

"I'm sure I'll find out," I laughed.

My parents' friends lived here and had kindly offered me a room. I told her the name of the street and she confirmed I was going the right way. I suppose once you've lived out of a rucksack, you become more aware of others attempting the same. You adopt a willingness to help out where possible, knowing it was at one time you that was lost or a bit unsure. We chatted all the way to my stop and past it, onto the next one. The short walk back though was worth it for a good first impression of the city of love.

Catherine and Tom had moved here 35 years ago, returning to Ireland often, so it was great to eventually take them up on their long standing invite. Another double bed was a thankful sight, as too was a hot shower. A great sleep later renewed my energy and curiosity, pushing me through the door, out to a sunny San Fran. I made it back into the city and caught a tram towards the numerous piers.

Again I had that familiar feeling. The old style tram, operated by a driver with a huge personality that matched his bulge, edged its way slowly up what seemed an impossibly steep hill. None of this a figment of Hollywood's imagination and a joy to experience. As we climbed, the view from similar steep side streets we passed, led to the ocean. I imagined the steeper a house sat on the hill, the fitter the home owner. Maybe the mortgage came with a fitness test and a heart scan. The driver loudly rang the tram's bell and like a trained actor, nailed his lines. Put on for the tourists no doubt, but it brought a smile to each of our foreign faces. I guessed he'd also seen the films, or they'd seen him. I hopped off the tram and walked to the wall that separated sea from land. The calm blue water of San Francisco Bay shone in the sunlight, the magnificent Golden Gate Bridge finding its way through it to my left and where I was headed now, Alcatraz sat still to my right.

I counted down to Pier 39, to where the tourist boats left daily for San Fran's main attraction. The seating area was left empty as we all lay out on the top deck, sun cream and cameras in hand. Once landed, our group was met by a tour guide to talk us through the several failed escape attempts during the prison's trading life. Dressed in a prison guard's uniform he talked with enthusiasm and experience, as if he'd spent time on the inside himself. Al Capone was famously imprisoned here in 1932, for none other than income-tax evasion. Entering the prison itself we were each given headphones and listened to directions and tales of how life was on the inside. Stepping into one of the cubicle sized cells reminded me of my stay in Hong Kong. I had spent only three nights but had felt the walls pressed tight, I couldn't imagine how it would feel faced with life, passing the days until death.

Back on the mainland I struggled to find an internet café. In Asia they had occupied most streets, their signs never further than a turn of your head. I suppose this was a city that could afford to put 'personal' into personal computers. Giving up my search to connect with the world, I decided a drink and the local gossip would do. I happened upon a pub quiz with a team in need of an extra brain and I spent the night trying to kick start mine.

The following day was Valentine's Day. What better place to be, I thought, than the city by the sea, the city of love. But without someone to lavish chocolates and flowers on, I'd have to entertain myself. The day was perfect for a cycle so I took my camera and rented a bike. The map provided highlighted surrounding areas of interest, but I knew where I wanted to go. I returned to the coast road and slowly made my way towards the Golden Gate Bridge. It wasn't long before I was positioned just short of and underneath its bulky steel frame. It had the appearance of rust proof paint neglect, but the sheer size gave you confidence in its very structure. I turned up a steep hill to twist and turn before appearing at the mouth of the metal sea creature. Cars covered the majority of the cement tongue, being swallowed and spat out too regularly to count. To the side, a footpath and cycle track ran, safely caged from the fast moving melee. As I cycled straight my head faced right, unable to take my eyes off where I had once been. Alcatraz shimmered in the sun, its beauty now daring me to forget what it held inside. To its right the city sat, hills escaping other hills, while tree-lined avenues played dot to dot to clarify its terrain. My progress was stop started by the changing angles my extending distance produced, each one worthy of being digitally frozen and later thawed out to frame.

Taking a right after clearing the bridge, dropped me down below the trees and I gathered speed then free-wheeled, legs apart, into Sausilito. This petite town eyes the city, its view obscured only by the floating prison. I locked my bike and walked its length, passing expensive boutiques and fancy restaurants. I picked one and dined on a tuna melt and two glasses of red wine, picking up details of lives I didn't know from well dressed older women at the table next to mine. This was my little treat and I was already smiling when the waitress winked at me as I paid the bill and left.

In the morning I set off in the car with Catherine and Tom to head north to Sonoma and Napa – wine country. Soon both sides of the road became manicured fields of vines as hundreds of wineries stretched out beside and beyond us. Any of these can be called on, and for only $10 their latest selection of wines can be tasted. Zinfandel is the main grape variety that is grown here, a gorgeous red that is bursting with flavours of blueberries and blackberries. It originated in Italy where the grape is known as a Primitivo, but once brought to California the Americans decided to rename it, better suited to their native slang.

We arrived at our first chosen winery before lunch and on near empty stomachs went about the tastings. After my third glass I could feel the effects. The slightly flushed sensation on my face, my heart rate increased, I imagined my lips were ruby in colour, and uncontrollable flirting with the waitress started.

This was certainly good stuff. Before each glass was poured, an explanation of its origin and life to date was given, and after each glass your opinion was asked. I was running out of sensible sounding syllables to string together and starting to think about a kebab, followed by a random snog and ending with a quick grope. Luckily, before I had the urge to strip and streak our ten-wine tasting was up. Lunch was then cleverly suggested before continuing to explore the mystery of the magic grape.

After our bite to eat we adopted a more sensible approach of occasionally spitting into the spittoon. I had to bless myself each time for the precious waste of alcohol. People had worked long and hard hours toiling in the fields under a burning sun to finally produce such tasty liquid and then I'd go and just spit it away. It wasn't right and I mentally noted a new low point in my life. Such are the wineries' popularity that hen and stag groups commonly rent a limo to drive them from winery to drunker and from drunker to winery for the day. I guess it was hit and miss which winery got the day's last visit. Ten flirtatious streakers, ruby lipped and kebab hungry enquiring about the depth and pungency of this year's crop is only fun if you are on the near side of the counter.

That night, dinner was arranged in a local restaurant. A send off and celebration I'd finally made it, all in one. Catherine and Tom's three sons were there, along with girlfriends and wives. The wine was Zin's, the food pizza and the laughs plenty. As we continued on to the local Irish Bar, I thought about how much I'd love to live here. It was my kind of city. Easy to get around and importantly plenty to do to make it worth getting around, with people who seemed to share my own outlook on life. The night changed colour as the small bar appeared to grow wings. Wine, women and song filled my senses as I gave into temptation and promised I'd return.

Take a walk down Main Street, on towards the Central Business Centre. Leave the skyscrapers behind that seem only to represent a very small part of this city and cross the street towards the water. It's here, on a grassy verge, between road and path, where you'll find my favourite place in San Fran. On a sunny day people stretch out on the grass, surrounding a giant bow and arrow that faces into the ground. Cupid's bow and arrow. The arrow's tip not to be seen, already penetrating the ground, piercing the heart that is San Francisco. I loved that image, that idea and now, this city.

San Diego

I boarded a Virgin flight San Diego bound. The soft purple neon hue that warmed the plane's inside reminded me of a massage parlour I had found in Beijing after a back realigning 15 hours on a Chinese sleeper bus. Lured in by a beautifully petite Asian girl with menace in her eyes, I was tortured for an hour by a large Hong Kong male with arms like pistons. The cabin crew seemed friendly enough to oblige me with a massage, had I asked, and beautiful enough to make it not last very long. This was a new route to Virgin's ever growing empire and although a small plane, it had all the comforts of one from their larger fleet. In contrast to our very own Ryanair, who sell only the illusion of cheap air travel until you land 100km from the advertised destination and pay out further for a bus to take you the rest of the way – this was first class. My only disappointment was the flight wasn't long enough. Virgin had managed to create a very comfortable and relaxing atmosphere in limited space. Ryanair make money from a gaudy, tacky fairground ride that should be scrap heaped. As for their trumpet self promotional jingle – shots should be fired at those responsible. Don't they know self praise is no praise?

I left the plane more relaxed than I am writing this, even bordering on lazy, so I found a taxi. I told the driver I was headed to the Banana Bungalow on Pacific Beach where Rossi had been holed up the last couple of weeks. Not that he was on the run, but you'd never know with him.

"You're Irish, right?" my transport technician inquired.

"I am," I said proudly.

"Aren't you a bit early then?"

I'm not sure I've been early for anything in my life, apart from getting out of bed unfortunately, which is usually way too early, so I was confused.

"All you Irish start to arrive here in May," he clarified.

San Diego had fast become an Irish student's playground in the sun, usually somewhere between the end of year exams and their repeats. Nothing like it to kill off a few more brain cells.

Like Rossi had said, a bed was booked in my name, in a dorm that already contained 15 other names. Situated right at the beach, this is one of the most popular hostels in town. Every morning a collection would be made for a cheap keg of beer and consumed on the decking. To the many passers-by it took on the appearance of a mad house rather then a budget bed boarder house. As I settled in, myself and Rossi caught up on the last two weeks and wondered what Brownie had gotten up to since our Auckland departure. We laughed as we recalled a story he had told us about his friend back home, who had an unusual way of chatting up women, if you could call it that. With a few drinks on board he'd position himself outside the women's toilet to propose a question as they exited. With all the confidence as if he was casually asking the time he'd say, "Good shit?"

Naturally, it apparently hadn't worked to date but the expressions were priceless. Now, excited about the night out that lay ahead of us, I waited to use the one small bathroom our room contained. An Irish girl eventually emerged and before I could stop myself, two four letter words slipped out. "Good shit?"

The expected shocked expression didn't materialise. As if relaying me the time, she said deadpan, "Yeah, it was actually."

I looked at Rossi, who was now deep in the depths of his rucksack to curtail his laughter, then looked back at the toilet. 101 delirious dalmatians couldn't have made me go in there now. We headed out earlier than planned.

Behind the hostel and in large orange lettering, Hooters declared its very existence. Much like applying a stamp before
posting a letter, we agreed we should eat before we drank. We
giggled our way to the door and entered expectantly, only to be
let down. This really was just a restaurant, a Planet Hollywood
like no other TGI's. Families filled the majority of the tables and
I'm pretty sure a kid's birthday party was in full swing down
the back. We lost the waitress lottery and got a man, then lost
our appetites and just got a starter.

Our stomachs were half full on chicken wings but half empty
for beer. The bar across the road complied to drinking standards that have been in play for decades – it was open. Having
availed of the pool table, we were shortly joined by others, one
being the most intense person I've ever met. He couldn't stand
still, choosing to practically run around the table after each
shot, barely waiting for the balls to settle. Questions weren't
as much asked, but drilled at you, as he tried to make sense of
why we were here in the first place. Without warning and often
in mid sentence, he'd run towards the bar, quickly returning
with more beers for us. I was convinced he was on a mixture of
cocaine and red bull and positive he was utterly useless at pool.
As he got more relaxed with us, if you can say that, he began
to talk more, like he was answering questions we hadn't asked.
In 30 seconds he summed up his life – he was in prison (reason
unknown), arrived in San Diego recently, remained unemployed
and above all that is pure, he basically needed a woman. By the
look on his face I figured he'd needed her since 2004. Another
glance in Rossi's direction would have confirmed agreement as
to what I was thinking, but he had already left.

A new bar is a new start in the life of an alcoholic – I'd imagine so anyway. The seal had been broken a few drinks back
which had dispatched Rossi to the toilet and me to the bar.
When I returned a young guy was in the same situation with
his friend.

"Do you wanna see a magic trick?" he started with.

"Sure I do," I said, interested.

With that, a length of rope was in his hands forming loops between his finger and thumb. With a series of twists he gave the illusion the rope had been snapped in two before revealing it still at full length. Before I could comment he was out with a selection of coins for his next trick, equally impressive.

"If you only had a pack of cards, I could show you one," I managed to get in.

With a smile he produced a deck.

"Are you a travelling magician?" I asked.

He laughed, "No sir, I'm a marine."

On the outskirts of San Diego lies a marine base. These two were on leave, spending it wisely. As a party of four now, we went from bar to bar, drinking and attempting magic tricks that understandably grew less graceful.

In the darkened hours I returned to my hostel dorm, felt my way around backpack obstacles, guessed right which bed was mine and fell asleep. When I awoke it was still dark, unusual I thought as that much drink generally sees me through to light. Then I realised what had woken me.

"7, 8, 9, 10, 11, 12, 13, 14."

Someone in the room was counting. Not slurred and quiet but pronounced and loud. I sat up in the bed and tried to focus into the night.

"20, 21, 22, 23, 24, 25," it continued.

I could make out the bed opposite now and the sleep counting offender. I dozed off again for what I knew was exactly 15 seconds, handy.

"41, 42, 43, 44, 45, 46, 47, 48."

That was enough to send me back to a deeper sleep wondering what the hell he was dreaming about.

The next morning, no one else had heard it and the sleep counter thought I was the one that was mad after I mentioned it.

Ah, the joys of hostel dorms!

There's a place, not far from here, I've always wanted to visit. Where people like to play games and when the Christmas lights are switched on, no one can tell. Where a lifestyle choice could leave you King of all below your penthouse suite or buried beneath a bed of sand. Where Elvis still lives to wed couples and where time keeping apparatuses have been made extinct. Easy to find your way in but near impossible to find your way out. Las Vegas.

Hotwire.com, a website I'd been told about, came in handy. Numbered flags identified where each hotel available was located. I filled in the boxes - 'Centre Strip' 'Cheapest' 'Four Nights'.

An agreeable price flashed up for a still nameless hotel. I entered my credit card details, ticked the box to confirm I was who I thought I was, and up popped my surprise.

"You are staying in.... The Flamingo."

Now, how to get there. Using the same website I clicked into the many cars available for selection. For as little as $35 a gorgeous red convertible Mustang was ours to travel through the desert in style. The morning would see the rental company handing me over the keys and wondering if they should be suspicious of the size of the grin on my face. They should.

Las Vegas

As soon as we broke free from San Diego, we shared the straight road with fellow thrill seekers. Vegas is a city that can deliver riches and we were all willing to take a chance. With the top down, the car's music stopped at our ears before being scattered like sand into the desert. The barren wasteland on either side was home only to snakes and scorpions. If you built a swimming pool, neatly laid out sunbeds and provided free towels, not even the Germans would show up. I suppose the real test would be to build a bar and see if any Irish arrived; I'd make it 50/50. Road signs indicated last remaining garages and advised switching off your air con to save fuel. This isn't a place to break down.

By mid afternoon, with the sun still in the sky, a chill in the air had turned on the car's heating and convinced me to buy a hat in the last garage. We gave it another hour before we ditched our idea of arriving onto Vegas' brightly lit runway with the top down. Otherwise we planned our entrance perfectly, coming within radio range just as the sun settled for the day. The sky was alight before the city was in sight. Batman would have an awful time here. With his Bat signal up against fierce competition, he'd have to rely on email or text messages.

'Holy haberdashery Batman, you got a voice mail!'

On the outskirts of the city we decided to refill the car's tank before we let it rest for a couple of days in the casino's parking lot. As I pulled into the garage I realised I had no idea what our rental ran on. Already in the forecourt though was a similar car to ours, the only difference was the colour and the better looking occupants. I knocked on the window, much to the four girls' amusement, and as I explained my predicament I could tell they were more interested in my accent than the possible danger to my car's engine.

"Where you from?" they asked.

We swapped information. I told them Ireland and they told me petrol.

Missing the turn for the car park I managed a U turn that more resembled an S as I avoided the oncoming gamblers making B lines for the slots. Not the best start, I thought, as Vegas is all about numbers rather than letters. After parking the car, we eventually found our escape from the mammoth car park over a series of walkways that led to a shopping mall, which turned out to be a wing of our hotel. Reception handed over our key and pointed us in the direction of the elevators, through the casino floor. Everything is cleverly planned here. Each time we'd leave and return to our room we'd have to pass through the casino floor – tables and slots. To eat, drink, change money, book a show, use the toilet or declare bankruptcy, we'd have to do the same.

The elevator's metal buttons shocked me twice before dispensing with me on my elected floor. There are over 150,000 hotel rooms in Vegas, that number greatly increasing when a new casino opens. The Flamingo alone has more then 3,500. To put it in some perspective, Dublin's celebrated Shelbourne Hotel has 265 rooms. To the average person like myself this means one thing; a hell of a long walk with your luggage to find your room. With everything else here so cleverly planned I'm sure a formula is used, summing up new arrivals to predict how much they'd gamble, this would then decide how close to the action they'd stay. I think my rucksack and worn Swedish T shirt gave me away as someone with a fast depleting budget. Apart from the distance, I couldn't complain about the room. Containing two large double beds and an even larger window, they had thoughtfully installed two sets of curtains to shield your sleeping eyes from the 24-hour light show beyond.

Returning to the casino floor I shied away from the tables. Never being much of a gambler or even a basic financial planner, I wasn't brave enough yet to face poker or ride roulette. Instead, I sat at the bar and proceeded to feed dollars into a computerised version of the same. The 'free drink if you're gambling' rule wasn't working out in my favour. I quickly said goodbye to $50 and had to almost manhandle a waitress in order to get two drinks. $25 a drink that cost $5. But like all around me I played into the illusion of free drink, that they cared, that I might possibly come up tops. Often, excited cries were heard from the gaming floor. The house was beaten and fresh possibilities infected each gambler's mind. A glance in their direction whetted your palate and unlocked your cash as gorgeous women draped over the winners like hungry cats. With nothing to show for it, I eventually found my way out of the Flamingo. Exits here are as hard to find as the time. They don't want you to leave and will gladly take your family fortune given the opportunity. Obscured by a field of slot machines, the door sat minuscule in the room of madness I had just left behind.

Out on the strip, innocent-looking kids handed out flyers for call girls. Similar magazines dirtied the paths where families walked. Sin City had everything on offer and was quick to dispense of any rules it didn't see fit for its idea of paradise. It was hard not to get sucked in, or as your gambles didn't pay off, buy into it. In one direction The Empire State Building and Eiffel Tower, another a giant pirate boat being attacked by suitably dressed trapeze artists. There wasn't a penny spared or, I assumed, a budget that hadn't been smashed to create this haven of possibilities. There was money here, a lot of it. In such a built-up area, crossing the road was no mean feat. Many of the casinos joined together though, your lucky slot machine possibly only a walkway away. For those who dare breathe fresh air a series of outdoor escalators and bridges shepherd you safely across the busy dual carriageway below. Thoughtful, but like everything here, preceded by a dollar sign. One person knocked down by a cash-filled transit van meant one less gambler on the floor – and we can't have that.

Unusually, unable to locate an Irish bar I decided on an Irish casino as the next best thing. Here the carpet was beer sticky, maybe another ploy to keep you within its doors, and the tables cheap, advertising a bet minimum of $5. I took a seat beside a woman with already a large mound of chips in front of her. A closer glance showed them up as only $5 chips. Not the high roller I had first thought, but then again neither was I. I cashed in $100 and immediately became more obsessed with the surrounding floor than the table, trying to eyeball a waitress into supplying me with drink. I chose roulette, having already a relative grasp of the rules, and fancied the 50/50 option of black or red. Even with this I failed to take advantage. Soon I was betting $40 to win back the $60 that had just disappeared. Once again the odds didn't go my way. The dealer gave me a knowing look. His time was spent disappointing most people who were betting money they shouldn't have been. I cashed in another $100 and my luck remained consistently unlucky.

"Maybe you should take a break," I heard the dealer say.

I looked up from my drink and saw that he was looking at me. His eyes were tired but soft. There was wisdom there. He had seen more than I, in a city he called home and a place I was just passing through. I squeezed the last from my glass, gave the dealer my remaining chip and walked away.

When I returned to my hotel I was unable to put a time on the place. A jazz band had just started up beside the gaming floor and the reception check-in queue seemed to be as long as earlier. The excitement absorbed me as I weaved through the tables so by the time I made it back to my room I wasn't tired.

In the morning we decided a round of golf would act as a suitable distraction for a few hours from the madness. We averted our eyes and managed to avoid temptation on the way to the hotel reception. When we announced our intentions, expensive-looking brochures for selected golf courses were placed in front of us. The prices quoted in the hundreds confirmed how they could afford such glossy bundles of advertising.

"We were wondering would you have anything cheaper?" I said meekly.

"Cheaper?" the receptionist replied, unhappy to even speak the dirty word in Vegas.

"Yeah, like maybe just a step up from pitch 'n' putt, a small step."

His attitude had cooled and his disdain told me he wondered what we were doing here in the first place.

"There is one, but it has no brochure, I will ring," he said dolefully.

"Sounds perfect."

Booked in, we set off with a roughly photocopied map and sprang our car free from its cavernous prison. The top stayed up as a rain cloud had positioned itself high above the desert floor, spitting drizzle but threatening more. Before I arrived in Vegas it appeared purely as a casino-filled strip in my head, my imagination fuelled by TV. Now, helplessly lost, the scale of the full blown city was upon me. The population of Vegas expands every year, most recently coming close to two million. We had been driving for 40 minutes and the area was still built up, not a grain of surrounding sand in sight. Two situations collided; we were lost, and it was lunch time. The golden arches of cheap food came into view promising to possibly solve both our problems.

"Could I get a Big Mac meal and some directions please?" I asked.

"Where you from?" she smiled.

"Ireland."

"Where?"

Now familiar with the way this conversation progressed I first mentioned Europe then closed it with England. With my burger meal in one hand she pointed with the other, directions I should follow. I hoped her local knowledge stood up to questioning and thanked her. As I walked away with my lunch I passed an older man eating and chuckling to himself. He had overheard our exchange.

"Sonny," he said as I grew near, " Geography isn't a very strong subject in this here neighbourhood."

When we returned to the car the threatened rain proved it wasn't empty. Eventually finding the course, they confirmed what we had feared; it was down for the day. Disappointed but not defeated we decided we'd check out the Hoover Dam that's built not far from the city. Buildings soon ceased to exist as barren rock once again spread out on both sides of the car. The straight tarmacked road was the only evidence of human activity. It rose and twisted its way down towards the tourist attraction. The dam crosses the border of two states, Nevada and Arizona, and interestingly, they are both part of different time zones. Walking across it I gained an hour then soon lost it again, clocks on either side confirmed my ability to time travel. Who needs a De Lorean?

Despite this I thought the dam itself was unimpressively small. In the valley though, just beyond, building had already begun on both sides of a new bridge. The height and distance through mid-air it would have to travel made for engineering genius. This seemed to sum up my experience of a lot of tourist attractions I had visited. The hype that builds them up and draws in the crowds serves to disappoint, but sometimes all you have to do is look in the opposite direction for the less obvious gem that makes it all worth while.

That evening, to stick with our day's theme of avoiding gambling our budget away, we opted to visit a well known strip club. We could sit at the bar and have a few drinks, we thought. The bouncers eyed us with suspicion, decided they could easily beat the biscuits out of us, then let us inside. To get to the bar it was like trying to cross the tempting casino floor. Gamblers and tables were replaced by strippers and couches. We both fell onto bar stools, knowing this was going to be harder than we thought. Our entrance had been noticed, word spread from the front line and reinforcements now emerged: appearing from a side door and landing on our laps. We had obviously caught them off guard because they hadn't finished getting dressed, in fact it seemed, they had barely just started. A stockinged leg tangled with mine, while a buxom blonde obscured my view of Rossi's noggin, seated beside me. The new view was a huge improvement all the same. I knew he had his own problems though, as the girl's questions were answered in a spate of giggles. I had to hand it to them, they had a way of making you feel special, like they had arrived for an evening of work only after several decades of the rosary were said, praying for the chance to dance for you that night.

300 girls work here, 100 were on tonight and one now had led me away from the bar for a dance. I didn't have to worry about making a fool of myself on the dance floor because for $10 only she got to dance and I just watched. A bit unfair, I thought. With the song over, another dance was suggested but this time somewhere more private and a lot more expensive. I mentioned my money issues and like a very exotic advert for AIB she draped herself over the nearby in house ATM. Just like

the casino, things could get out of hand real quick here. I noticed Rossi was in a similar pickle. It was time to leave, frustrated, but with some of our budget left.

Before checking out the next morning, I needed to sort a flight to New York, so I found internet access in the casino's business centre. A slit for your credit card made it obvious it would take Mr. Visa just to check your email. A bit unsure, I provided my card and the web was mine. Not knowing how much was being extracted from my bank account by the second I quickly searched and made decisions. With a final click I swiped my card back and a receipt was printed off. My few minutes on line had cost me $25. You'd want to be making million dollar deals or win big to justify the use of it.

"Hi honey, just wanted to let you know I got lucky last night on the slots. Love you."

"Hi honey, sorry, half of it is gone!"

"Me again, ring the bank, we need a loan."

We left Vegas tired. Not easy to live up to its huge scale, it takes it out of you. Friends who had been there previously had said three or four days there is enough. They were right. A night in Barstow facilitated sleep without temptations, nothing else, and the following day we were back where our road trip had started, San Diego. Gone was our red mustang. Gone was my imagined perception of Vegas. Gone was more of my budget. Gone was Rossi. New York, here I come.

New York

After flying through the night, I landed in Philadelphia. The two-hour wait in the airport for my connecting flight passed with the night sky gradually becoming brighter. Without delay, the small 30-seater plane entered the early morning to take the remaining few of us on to New York City. In an open-eyed daze I leaned against the window, my head cushioned only by my hand, my body too tired to care about the discomfort. In a short time the plane started to descend through the blanket of cloud that seemed to divide night from day. Wisps of white fluff edged past me outside. When the plane cleared the covering, we were above Manhattan. Connections were made within my brain as my eyes relayed what they were seeing and the information instantly affected my whole body. I sat bolt upright and suddenly having only the two eyes as standard for humans wasn't nearly enough. I explored the different angles my porthole would allow and strained against my seatbelt for release. Although dull from the weather, the skyscrapers defined the city's look, undeniably proud and strong willed. With the further drop in altitude I could make out the snow-dashed streets and escaping steam, as the heat from the underground pipes discovered how cold it was above ground. The plane banked to line up with the runway. I had an appetite for breakfast and a hunger to walk the streets my porthole had teased me with.

I spent the last seven months following the sun, watching as it retired for the night; it was there in the morning to gradually heat my bones until I woke. As I stepped through the airport's sliding doors, a blast of man-made heat was followed by the day's harshness, and the realisation that I was considerably under-dressed. The warmest clothes I had were a worn pair of jeans and a hoodie. I would have to shop appropriately if I was to survive the coming week. I quickly jumped into the warmth of a yellow cab and directed the driver to 59th Street, where I had booked a bed in the Continental Hostel – breakfast not included.

After settling in, I excitedly set off, catching an amused look from the receptionist, no doubt in reference to my current clothing. The heavens had decided to open, but not to hand Moses a couple of tablets, this time it was to throw snow, hail and rain in my direction. Within a block I resembled a wet sock. Like the sighting of land to lost sea-crazed Spanish, I spotted the first of a line of street stalls and hope was restored. An umbrella was in hand and a woolly hat head-height by the first – a scarf, gloves and coat soon followed. I was ready to take on the city.

I had developed a nerdy passion for maps since booking my first flight to leave my familiar streets. I loved reading the unusual place names and trying to gauge distances between countries. On the more compact city maps every street name appeared as a possible adventure. New York's grid style format makes for easy negotiation, or so I thought. Referring to my local bought pocket-sized street map was getting me completely lost. When I thought I was going East, it was West – presuming North, I was wandering South. I'd only notice my mistake after I'd walked a block. I came to the conclusion the misprinted map needed to be read up-side-down and through a mirror. I didn't mind all the same, with nowhere in particular to be, I was never late not to be somewhere else.

I walked through Central Park, where people found refuge from the chaos beyond, and on to Greenwich, with its beautiful tree-lined quiet side streets. Small café shops and bars interspersed with homes and even the fallen leaves seemed to have a special place here. I found a pizza shop to see if they'd measure up to all I'd heard. The two slices I'd ordered were like whole pizzas themselves and although mouthwatering I struggled to finish. To wash it down, with the little space I had left, I found a café bar with live music. Once again I was amazed with the standard on show. This would be a very hard city to make it for the aspiring songwriter.

Having enjoyed the music and wine I found my subway line and headed home. The half an hour underground had developed in me a further thirst, so I decided on one more in the local bar. Straight away the barman embraced me with conversation and as I bought my second beer, he said the next was on him. Soon a third person arrived and talk continued. Now, seated beside me, leather clad, tattoo tagged and head shaven, was a self proclaimed true New Yorker. All 6 foot 6 of him. He asked questions and listened with great interest to my previous months discovering the world we live in.

"Wow, well, now I want to show you my city," he said with a booming enthusiasm.

"John," I replied, extending my hand.

"Wayne."

The morning had lifted the rain but turning a corner the wind chill could still cut you in two. I walked to the site of the once standing World Trade Centre. Now reduced to a hole in the ground, the whole area was fenced off as building work had begun. The workmen reminded me of Doozers from Fraggle Rock, looking down on their yellow hard hats as they built up the foundations for the replacement. There was a very eerie feel to the place, like stumbling across an unexplained square of grass in the middle of a tree-filled forest. I then continued on to The Empire State Building to take in the great views it provided. As I was leaving my phone rang.

"John, it's Wayne, man, where are you?"

"Just leaving the Empire State."

"Great, I'm on 5th in a black van."

"See you in a sec so," I said, as I second thought my decision on how to best explore the city.

I have no doubt, if you want to really see a place, the best thing you can do is hook up with a local, but as I crossed the road towards a black van containing a lookalike extra from Mad Max, I was having doubts.

"We'll start at Woodlawn, what I call 'Irish Town'," Wayne said, "everything is Irish."

We joined the busy traffic, stop-starting over our small talk.

"So I went to see the site of the World Trade Centre this morning," I began, "must have been weird living here when that happened."

"Eh, I was away," Wayne replied.

"Cool, on holiday, where did you go?"

"No man, I was put away, the cops caught up with me."

Conversation killer. I was so tempted to ask why, but figured an hour at a bar and five minutes in his van hadn't qualified me as a mate.

"Mmm, what do you work at?" I tried.

He shifted positions. I could tell that wasn't a good question to get the conversation flowing again.

"We'll say, catering," he said through the side of his mouth directed towards me.

Maybe sensing a change of atmosphere was needed or the time had already come to be rid of me, he swerved to the side of the road.

"Get out," he said looking right at me.

"What," I stuttered after a pause.

"C'mon man, best hot dogs in town here, my shout."

I laughed at myself, over thinking once again.

Wayne loved his city, nearly as much as the chance to prove it and show it off to someone like me. After a gorgeous hot dog, he talked as he drove, pointing when he could, reeling off facts he'd grown up with, all around him. As he had suggested, we turned a corner and drove down the main street of Woodlawn. The street seemed to have been airlifted from Connemara and landed in New York's suburbs. Every shop, butchers and bar proudly displayed an Irish surname and the painted green was more common than the bricks that built them. We continued to drive until we reached water, then proceeded on foot down a wooden pier.

"Look at that man," Wayne said pointing, "that's New Jersey."

Off in the distance, past the water, inches of land could be seen, like a piece of black duct tape that separated the water from the start of the sky. Wayne stared out as if he was transfixed by the glow of the Aurora Borealis, staying silent, giving off the air of appreciation for open spaces of a man once confined. The mood was broken by his phone ringing. I was privy to half the conversation, trying to hide my smile as I guessed the rest.

"Sup man?" Wayne started.

"Well, did you do anything?"

"Who you been hanging with these days?"

"Don't leave your place until I ring back, I'll make calls and find out what's going down."

He hung up and muttered to himself, "damn cops."

It seemed in this city the cops were pretty good at catching up to those who preferred to remain uncaught.

We climbed back into the van leaving New Jersey untouched. I had earlier mentioned that on my 'to do' list while in New York, was to pick up some presents. Although I also insisted I could sort this in my own time, Wayne insisted even more he wanted to help out, so our next stop would be a shopping mall. As we pulled in within walking distance, Wayne reached into the glove compartment and produced a previously rolled joint.

"Let's have this first," he declared with a menacing smile.

Conversation ceased completely as we both withdrew to our own worlds, our heads lifting momentarily to render our bodies mute and lazy. I had to force myself out of the seat to follow Wayne who had just taken off without word of warning towards the shops. We must have looked like the odd couple on grocery reconnaissance. I did my best to look through racks of shirts and trousers, not knowing if they were for men or women, nothing registering with me, least of all my purpose for being there in the first place. I floated from aisle to aisle, losing Wayne, before nearly walking into him and a basket of discount slippers. Shopping had never been so surreal. He had picked out a shirt and tie which I couldn't get my head around and I doubted would even fit around his neck. I wondered had he really thought through his future purchase or was his current status persuading him to become a bank manager. Then again, maybe there was a court appearance pending. As I stood awkwardly mid aisle, unable to pretend I was shopping any more, he followed through and bought them. I made some excuse for my lack of purchases and we found our way back to the van. Happy to sit down again, I closed my eyes. As the ill effects wore off, Wayne dropped me to the subway. I thanked him for the tour, declared I'd do the same if he ever made it to Dublin and made a mental note that if he did, I'd have to find a dealer.

"John," he shouted after me.

I turned and saw his head and rugged arm framed where the door's window once was.

"If anyone fucks with you let me know, this is my city."

I think he had waited for some distance to increase the dramatics. The few other people in earshot didn't seem interested.

"Thanks man," I smiled back, and with my thumb still in the air he drove off to sort out his mate's newly risen problems.

My week in New York had disappeared, much like my last months, leaving me with random snippets continuously popping in and out of my head. People, I would relate to places, and bars, I would relate to hungover sightseeing. It was like I had lost my memory and it was slowly reappearing as a muddled jigsaw, waiting for me to sit down and piece it all together. One giant colourful picture or a continuous flow of words – a book. JFK airport remains a blur, a piece of jigsaw lost under the couch. Now confused with numerous other arrivals and departure lounges: Singapore, LA, Sydney. I did board a plane though, and it took me away from the States, closer to home, to London.

Chapter 11

BED & BAR

London

L ondon has always done it for me. Previous visits would start out as a weekend away and turn into a bank account-breaking week as I refused to get my allotted return flight. There was always so much to do and see I didn't want it to end. I hadn't checked my bank balance while in New York, I was afraid to, I knew it wasn't good, and reality loomed on the horizon. After spending the last few months changing the dates of my flights without a second thought, I now knew when I'd arrive back in Dublin.

Landing in Heathrow, one change on the underground brought me to East London where I had booked the cheapest room I could find that was still in walking distance of a tube station. It was above a bar, so well within sleeping distance of last orders too. Leaving the station, I searched the walls for a street name to gather my bearings. Above a kebab shop, weather-worn but still in place, I spotted 'Green Street'. It made a connection somewhere in my head and as I walked in the direction of my Bed & Bar (who needs breakfast?) it bounced around between my ears like they were enjoying a game of old style computer tennis. One of them scored an ace as a football ground came into view on my left and I read the words 'West Ham' – game over. My brain pin-pointed the connection to a film I had seen on football hooligans, and in general, what all round nice people they were not.

With a steady pace I found the Central Bar, keen to ditch my rucksack and anything else that identified me as a new arrival. It wasn't yet lunchtime when I entered the bar, the dull lighting pleased my tired eyes, but the stale smell of the beer-soaked carpet took up occupancy in my nose. The two paying customers already present paid me no attention, both consumed in their own worlds of eating breakfast with a pint and cajoling a brightly lit slot machine into defeat. I told the woman behind the bar I had a room booked for three nights.

"Cash or card, love?" she smiled through smoke-stained teeth.

"Card, thanks," I replied handing over the rectangular piece of plastic that had shown me the world without letting me down.

"It's declined, love." Until now.

"Really? Eh, okay, cash then," I said more disappointed than shocked.

The inevitable had happened, you can't argue with that. I scraped together what was needed and waited until I was within my new four walls to count what was left. Subtracting the cost of the underground to Liverpool St. and a connecting train to Luton Airport, not to mention the Aircoach bus from Dublin Airport home, things were bad. As I looked around my room, only big enough for a bunk bed and a miniature kettle, I loved it. The sense of freedom I still had in my firm grasp was mine for the next few days, and anyway, money isn't a prerequisite for enjoyment.

I left the bar and ventured back into the city. Something in my head was willing me to return to where I had first stayed all those years ago. Maybe it was the desire for something famil-iar after the months spent wandering and stumbling in the un-known. The underground's serrated metal teeth lifted me stead-ily to Russell Square beyond. I spent the day walking on towards Leicester Square and Covent Garden, remembering bars I drank in and friends I had met. Jill from Melbourne popped back into my head. It was here I'd met her, years before, one person in a city of millions and she had managed to repeat it a second time. Maybe that meant something, maybe not. I stopped in a bar for a drink and was soon in conversation with an English guy who was there before catching a train home after his day's work in the city. When it was time for him to leave, he was insistent I took his number and got in touch, as his girlfriend's birthday was coming up with a party I shouldn't miss. The friendliness and general sincerity in others was something I had become accustomed to at this stage and, with it, grew my trust. I just hoped I continued to feel the same in Dublin.

As I made my way towards the underground station that would return me to Green Street, I was stopped by a camera crew.

"Can we ask you a quick question?" the mike-wielding pretty girl asked.

"Sure."

"Patrick Swayze is reportedly dying, what is your opinion on this?"

I laughed out loud, looking straight into the camera lens. It appeared downright heartless but the question hit me just like the old work question had in Bangkok, or my friend back home wondering how my weekend went while I was lost in a Vietnamese time zone. Out of context it didn't make sense, but it wasn't that the question was out of context, it was me. I felt I was now out of context with the rest of the world. I hadn't been reading the newspapers so I was completely out of touch with anything that was happening outside the price of hostels or must-see temple ruins. The girl looked at me, obviously disgusted. I tried to drag my brain back into the real world but failed dramatically with a single word, 'footloose'.

"I'm sorry," I tried, "I just haven't been around for a while."

"Okay," she said, no doubt thinking of mental asylums or prison possibilities to explain my weirdness. I continued to walk, smiling to myself, but an undercurrent of worry emerged. How was I going to manage being back home?

On my way to my room I stopped at the bar. I could afford a drink and wasn't yet ready to be on my own. It was busier than it had been this morning and this time I could feel eyes focus to my attention. My Irish accent was heard as I ordered a pint and curiosity was roused as to why I was there, clearly off any tourist or backpacker's route. To a group of three men I explained how London had spring-boarded me around the globe only to catch me once again with considerably less money, in fact, none. While ordering me a drink, they each recalled their own stories. Leaving Dublin decades before, London had cocooned them to this day. Rarely returning to Irish soil, this was their home now. As they continued to buy me drink I got the feeling it was their way of reaching out with two hands to their birthplace or else, in me, they saw a little of their young selves, only I'd taken a step further. Whatever the reason, I wasn't complaining.

Then, without warning, the mood in the bar changed, a slight edge seemed to infringe on the relaxed. Through the crowd I saw a grey-haired man making his way towards us. Although short in stature, people parted from his way without a second thought. His oversized brown leather jacket made him look bulkier than he was. When he made it over to our little group, his cold eyes locked onto the unfamiliar: me.

"This is John," one of his friends spoke up on my behalf, "he's Irish and he's been travelling."

"Hello," he said coldly and firmly shook my hand.

He reminded me of Don Baker in the movie 'In the Name of the Father', who played the part of a psychopathic IRA bomber who would charm you one minute before stabbing you through the eye with his toothbrush the next. It wasn't just his appearance, it was the silent respect that bordered on fear he had brought to the room. Even his friends now appeared unsure, waiting his approval on how to proceed.

"Where were you?" his eyes never leaving mine.

I briefly repeated my story, his friends nodded along to a silent accompanying soundtrack. When I had finished, he bought me a drink. As he turned in towards the bar he motioned for me to do the same. In a hushed tone, he told me he was also Irish but hadn't been back in nearly 30 years.

In an attempt to lighten the mood I said, "ah sure, the flights are so cheap nowadays."

"I can't go back," he said flatly.

I knew the reason wasn't that he couldn't find the road to the airport. Don Baker's image returned to my head, so too did Wayne's. When was I going to learn to stop putting my foot in it when engaged in conversation with various possible gang members?

As the drinks continued to be bought for me and consumed, his intensity started to soften. He oddly liked that we shared the same name and, as we discovered, we both played guitar. This appeared to be connection enough and after awhile he leaned in my direction and asked me to step outside with him. Crossing the bar I wondered had he brought his toothbrush. I was still very happy about getting my eyes lasered before leaving home. I liked my eyes. Once outside he looked in both directions to make sure we were alone, or else he was just making sure we were really outside, I couldn't tell, but he could have just asked because I knew we were.

"I'm going to give you my number," he said quietly.

Before I could respond he continued.

"You can come back over and stay in one of my properties, I'll sort you out with work. Oh, and bring your guitar."

I was pretty sure I hadn't hinted at residing in London any time soon. He continued to look at me in-between quick checks of both ends of the street, like his head had a nervous tic. I felt like I was being recruited for a gang of underground freedom fighters opposed to pea farmers, that or the IRA. I wasn't sure how to react so I took out my phone and he started to pronounce each number steady and deliberate, a bit like he was sleep counting. Five digits in and the bar door swung open, ejecting a couple of smokers to where it was legal. John stopped dead and once again turned to stone, the same tension as earlier reappearing in the outdoor arena. No effort of conversation was made, we just waited. When the cigarette butts were dropped in the street and the door used again, he looked up at me but his tone made me feel smaller.

"No one must know that I've given you my number."

"Of course, no worries," I reassured him. Well, I made the effort anyway.

Back inside, the karaoke machine had come to life with a local murdering a Robbie Williams number. More drinks were bought and placed in front of me. I was well on the way to an early morning of extreme thirst and had only bought a single drink. John leaned in towards me again.

"Right, now we sing and we sing good."

I figured it wasn't a good time to mention I was vocally challenged when it came to anything but talking. I followed him towards the stage as people instinctively parted to introduce open carpet space. He handed me the second mike, having already selected a song. I just hoped I knew it. I wondered were rebel songs available in karaoke format and if they were, would this really be a safe place to let rip? The music started up. To my surprise I did know it but thought maybe the DJ had selected the wrong track. I turned to face John and found my answer. His brown leather jacket was attached to him by only one arm now, as he swung it in circles above his head. His face was lit up with youthful excitement and the packed bar egged on where their full attention was now focused. Then the singing started.

'You can dance, you can jive, having the time of your life, see that girl, watch that scene, digging the Dancing Queen.'

I jumped in as soon as my brain got to grips with the bizarre situation unfolding on stage. The feared hard man had himself turned into a dancing queen, expressing each beat, word and sentence with limb movements I thought were only possible by Ecuadorean tribeswomen. His jacket dangled from his wrist, the rest of his body unaware now of its latest attachment. His enthusiasm infected me as I began to sing with facial expressions Celine Dion would have been proud of. As the song ended the next began and we continued for a further three numbers.

The call for a beer eventually ended our mini gig, where we had gone from novelty to annoyance with the crowd. John was on a high, his hard man persona temporarily dropped, rounds for the rest of the night were on him. We hurdled over midnight and landed in the next day's morning. The bar called an end to things by calling time and my goodbyes were received with hugs. John's grip was as firm as his original handshake.

"I'll see you soon then," he said, "don't forget your guitar."

I zig-zagged my way up the stairs and through the corridor, falling fully clothed on my bed to sleep. That night I dreamt of peas.

My remaining days were spent travelling underground, coming up for air at places called Notting Hill, Camden Town, Clapham and Tooting. I had no plan as such. These couple of days felt like my last meal before I'd be marched off down a corridor into a room for a nice sit down. Fortunately my death wasn't next on the agenda, just an end to my travels for the time being, a return home. It all came too soon though. The city was in my wake as I argued with the girl at the Ryanair check-in desk over the weight of my luggage. Having a personality doesn't seem to be part of the required skills to obtain such a job.

"You need to pay 40 pounds, sir," her mouth managing to move despite being caked in make-up on either side and sealed with red lipstick.

I really hate that, when they add in 'sir' at the end of a sentence. Like they could say anything to you but by adding 'sir', the false respect gets them away with it.

"That will be an additional €450 for the extra petrol we'll need to use since your luggage is well overweight and you should really think about losing a couple of stone too.... sir."

Right then I wanted to tell the smug bitch with her yanked back hair in a granny bun where she could stick her 'sirs', her attitude and her talk of anything being overweight. Instead, I counted out pennies and paid, knowing damn well I could shoot off her left ear right there and she'd still remain zombie-like and refer to me as 'sir'. I was back in a part of the world where an apparent cheap flight gets you no service or manners at all and it's implied we should be grateful. For some reason we put up with it.

The short flight was forgettable, which is your best tactic with a Ryanair flight because if you remember anything, you'll just get pissed off. Dublin's weather hadn't changed even though I had left in August; rain still persisted and cloud still covered. It was reflected on the people's faces. Home life, job satisfaction, loving and being loved; none of these appeared to be reasons for happiness any more. It was all down to the weather. I realised this was the first airport I'd landed in recently without a state of excitement, without a curiosity, and without a smile on my face. Here in Dublin Airport though, I soon blended in, my demeanour had changed, my tanned skin the only give-away.

I was home.